DEVELOPMENT AND UNDERDEVELOPMENT

DEVELOPMENT AND UNDERDEVELOPMENT

The History, Economics and Politics of North-South Relations

HARTMUT ELSENHANS

SAGE Publications
New Delhi/Newbury Park/London

FOR HILDEGART

First published in 1984 by Verlag W. Kohlhammer as *Nord-Süd Beziehungen: Geschichte-Politik-Wirtschaft* (German). Translated by Madhulika Reddy.

This edition published in 1991 by
Sage Publications India Pvt Ltd
M-32, Greater Kailash Market, I
New Delhi 110 048

Sage Publications Inc
2455 Teller Road
Newbury Park, California 91320

Sage Publications Ltd
6 Bonhill Street
London EC2A 4PU

Published by Tejeshwar Singh for Sage Publications India Pvt. Ltd, photo-typeset by Jayigee Enterprises and printed at Chaman Offset Printers.

ISBN 0-8039-9679-9 (US-hbk)
          0-8039-9680-2 (US-pbk)
          81-7036-222-9 (India-hbk)
          81-7036-223-7 (India-pbk)

Contents

List of Abbreviations

GATT	General Agreement on Tariffs and Trade
GNP	Gross National Product
IMF	International Monetary Fund
LDC	Less Developed Country/Underdeveloped Country
MNC	Multinational Corporation
NIEO	New International Economic Order
OPEC	Organisation of Petroleum Exporting Countries
SITC	Standard International Trade Classification
UN	United Nations
UNCTAD	United Nations Conference on Trade and Development
UNDP	United Nations Development Programme
UNIDO	United Nations Industrial Development Organisation

Preface to the English Edition

Since the first German edition of the book, the new ascendancy of liberalism in development theory and its critical stand against the state of development in the Third World has seemed to render outmoded the reflection on North–South relations. These relations lend themselves to critical assessment only if the opening up of economies to the world market is considered as not automatically leading to economic progress in the South. In fact, development theory has its origin in a Keynesian world of imbalance economics, blocked from harmonious growth. It was thought that backward areas, as the Third World was originally called, should necessarily be developed by planned state interventionism. State responsibility and state interventionism became generalised in the South from the 1930s, first in Latin America, then in the newly independent countries of Asia and, even before decolonisation, in the late-colonial strategies of Britain and especially France in Africa.

The financing of new investment required resources as long as additional productive capacity was built up through the import of investment goods. The growth process in the Third World was considered to be dependent on 'capital'—defined as foreign exchange for the purchase of equipment. Therefore, two main aspects of development theory emerged: Determining the most appropriate strategies for channelling resources into growth through the state, and developing ways to increase the amount of resources. Controversies about strategies of industrialisation and attempts at changing the international distribution of purchasing power dominated development theory, whether it stressed more state control over the economy and especially over external economic relations, or whether it stressed greater integration into the capitalist world system. The demand for a new international economic order was the logical outcome of such strategies. Debates on underdevelopment generated by the transfer of resources from the South to the West—in the past or even at present—were the natural theoretical underpinnings of these types of state-guided development strategies.

The crisis of the 1980s led to a shift in emphasis. State interventionism and self-centred development came more and more under theoretical attack. State interventionism and import-substituting industrialisation were increasingly considered to be responsible for slow growth and rising indebtedness. More trade, more direct foreign investment, and encouraging export-led industrialisation were considered appropriate policies for overcoming underdevelopment, despite the serious drawbacks involved in such strategies.

However, both theoretical perspectives—i.e., state-guided, state-financed, inward-looking strategies, and world market oriented export promotion—ignore the crucial problem of the social preconditions for overcoming underdevelopment. In the first approach, development is considered to be the outcome of investment. Development occurs through the purchase of investment goods which will result in a diversification of the economy. This strategy finally leads to increased technological and financial dependence, although it is meant to result in a greater measure of delinking from the world market. The second approach considers integration into the world market as the main vehicle of growth, which—like investment in the first case—is believed to bring about changes in the social structure and the pattern of income distribution by economic automatism. As these automatisms are very weak in an increasingly impoverished Third World, the West tries to protect itself against the nearly unlimited supply of cheap labour in the South, which erodes the bargaining power of its working class. Export promotion is accepted only half-heartedly by the industrial countries of the West. Although differing in their practical approaches, both strategies are almost similar in terms of their basic theoretical framework: Development is the result of an accumulation of capital financed, in the first case, through state mobilisation of local savings and state control of external economic relations (raw material prices, foreign direct investment, aid, debt), and in the second case, through the pull of exports and the inflow of export earnings. The theoretical perspective of this book is a different one, capable of explaining the shortcomings and failures of both strategies.

Although economic development is certainly connected with investment, the fundamental aspect is that investment is linked to expanding markets for machine-made goods. In addition, if an economy develops the capacity to produce machinery, there is no lack of resources for financing such development. Nobody will, however, order new machinery if markets for machine-made products do not exist, or do not expand. Capitalism and development are, therefore, linked to egalitarianism and rising mass incomes.

Western mainstream economics have tended to insist on investment, capital accumulation, and inequality (in order to raise the saving rate) because the Western working classes generated appropriate increases in mass demand without taking recourse to economics.

Orthodox Marxists had to deny rising mass incomes as a precondition for capitalist growth in order to maintain their rejection of the possibilities for reforming capitalism. Keynesianism, as evolved within the framework of developed capitalist systems, insisted on the state's role in regulating business cycles and did not spell out its implications for long-term growth.

As technical efficiency does not increase in proportion to the amount of labour devoted to producing machinery but on the basis of knowledge and experience in production, late-comers to machinery production will be comparatively disadvantaged in machinery production. Besides, the requirement of expanding internal mass markets is even more important for them than it was for the earlier industrialists due to the following reasons: High income groups in the Third World of today have high import propensities even if they consume industrial products, whereas high income groups among the earlier industrialists could consume either locally produced industrial products or imported handicraft items. Moreover, products manufactured locally for high income groups in today's Third World require more sophisticated and, therefore, a higher quantum of imported technologies than is the case with products consumed by the mass of the population.

The first chapter of this book reiterates the link between mass consumption and development, and criticises the world system perspective developed by some Marxist authors. The West did not develop through the exploitation of the South, but by its own means. This, however, led to the exploitation of the South. Without rising mass incomes, unequal specialisation and low labour costs in the South resulted in low prices for its products.

The second chapter demonstrates how unequal specialisation and the deformation of the economies of the South resulted—as a consequence of the spontaneous economic tendencies they triggered off, as well as the political reaction in the societies of the South against underdevelopment—in a specific class structure and a specific mode of production, which I call a bureaucratic development society. This specific mode of production is characterised by the domination of State–classes. They are in control of the major part of the economic surplus. They are liberated from the 'law of value' and are, therefore, immune to sanctions against them, even if they invest in nonprofitable undertakings. They may commit themselves to strategies of overcoming underdevelopment through mass consumption, but there is no economic and political mechanism forcing them to do so. And even when they adopt such strategies, implementation is difficult. But it has been maintained, against the liberal view that the necessary emergence of rent in underdeveloped countries makes these State–classes the potential promoters of progress.

The third chapter shows that if reorientation of the productive apparatus to mass needs is not achieved, any strategy of economic development will fail, whatever be its stand on particular issues such as external economic relations, type of technologies, priority of sectors, etc. Export-oriented industrialisation will have too low an impact to clear the labour markets in the South. Import-substitution will avoid new dependency on foreign technology only if it is geared to expanding mass markets and local technology production. Multinational enterprise will continue to contribute to monopolisation and profit remittances, if local mass markets do not expand and create new outlets for investment. Increased earnings from raw materials and increased resources from international lending can only be utilised for overcoming underdevelopment if the internal social setup is changed.

In the fourth chapter, the demand of the Third World for a new international economic order is reviewed. It is shown that results achieved have been limited and that the issue has been put forward in an incomplete manner: A further transfer of resources is conducive to overcoming underdevelopment if it is linked to a restructuring of the productive apparatus to mass needs. Such a restructuring would be in the interest of the working classes of the West. The West, however, denies new resources, and the State–classes of the South are not committed to social reform.

In the fifth and concluding chapter, a scenario for a reform-oriented alliance between social forces in the West and in the South is presented. In my view, such an alliance is necessary, if a liberal world economy is to survive.

Since the first German publication of the book, the tendencies to be expected in the absence of such a reformist alliance have been aggravated. The indebtedness of the South has mounted, even though austerity measures were taken. In some countries, sovereignty has been virtually abolished by policies of structural adjustment. Repayment of the debt, even though not desirable from the point of view of maintaining global demand, is hampered by barriers to access to Western markets. Moreover, access to Western markets will fail to cause additional unemployment in the West only if Western markets expand. Most Western governments view increases in mass income as a threat to the competitiveness of their export industries. A mutual race in cost reduction through wage restraint reinforces deflationary tendencies in the West. This had led to erosion of the prices of raw materials (lack of demand), declining international lending (decline in credit-worthiness of the Third World), limited aid (decline in tax revenue of the governments of industrial countries) and protectionism.

Confronted with this behaviour on the part of the West, the solidarity of the South has vanished. The demand for a new international economic order put forward by the South has been replaced by demands from individual countries for debt relief, preferential aid and access to markets. In order to obtain such concessions, they offer a reduction in the role of the State and weaken thus, the necessary instrument for restructuring their economies. Unintentionally, the crisis in external resources propels more self-reliance in the industrially more advanced countries, as import capacity declines. But the growing differences in development do not obliterate the objective unity of the Third World, even though a few countries succeed in quitting the Third World as their industries diversify. This has been linked to the successful development of their internal mass markets and a conscious attempt to engage in machinery production, even if initially of low quality (South Korea, Taiwan). But even the major part of the newly industrialising countries will remain dependent on imported technology and will not be able to expand their local mass markets. If, due to economic expansion in the West, exports should resume, the old incentives for not undertaking to overcome underdevelopment will, once again, operate and will deepen underdevelopment, as did the lack of financial resources during the crisis. The necessity of a concerted approach to overcoming underdevelopment by linking a new international economic order to social reforms in the South will continue to exist.

Konstanz
October 1989.

H.E.

Preface to the
First Edition

Since the sixties, international relations have undergone a change. Beside the rivalry between the two superpowers of the North for military security, exemplified in the arms race, there has emerged the North–South conflict. This new aspect of 'international politics' is, however, predominantly neither a relationship between the North as a whole and the South, nor a purely political relationship. For that matter, it is hardly even a conflict in its primary sense. *North–South relations are principally West–South relations.* The South exports twenty times the volume of goods to the Western industrialised countries than it does to the USSR and the countries of Eastern Europe. It imports ten times as much from the West as from the East. Development aid from the West is a good twenty times of that from the East. In fact the West constitutes virtually the only source of credit, direct investment and technology for the South. This dependence of the South on the West, as indicated by these observations, has resulted in the fact that problems of the distribution of international wealth constitute the central issue in West–South relations.

Since no aid can be expected from adversaries, the South does not wish to antagonise the West; instead, it seeks to meet its objective by demanding changes in the conditions governing economic co-operation with the West. These conditions, a crucial topic in North–South relations, have their origins in the very genesis of the capitalist world–economy in the sixteenth century. There are many in the Third World who attribute the poverty and the underdevelopment of the South to the latter's incorporation into this world economy, virtually controlled as it was, and still is, by Western Europe and North America. At the same time, this link between the West and the South brought about changes in the social structures of the

South. Many developing countries have witnessed the emergence of new social forces seeking to overcome underdevelopment. In the process, they encounter problems relating to external trade, which they attempt to resolve by submitting demands to the West.

It is these complexities in North–South relations that form the subject of this book, whose main thesis runs as follows:

The industrial countries of the West too have a stake in the New International Economic Order (NIEO), even if it is the poor of the Third World who stand to really gain by this order. Just as poverty and underdevelopment are not merely consequences of the unequal division of labour and, historically speaking, of the South's discrimination at the hands of the West, so also underdevelopment too cannot be overcome merely by reaching agreements in the sphere of West–South economic relations. Reforms should be effected within the countries of the South itself.

If, on the other hand, poverty is not overcome in the South, then the West will find itself more and more incapable of solving its own economic problems: At the close of the millennium, there would probably be around seven hundred million unemployed from the developing countries on the international labour market who, as a result of international economic linkages, will increasingly displace the active labour force of the Western industrialised countries. The danger of downward equalisation looms ahead, if poverty in the South is not surmounted through rising employment opportunities and growing mass incomes.

In this connection, I wish to thank Ms. Rose Kopf, Ms. Brigitte Späth and Mr. Harald Fuhr for the assistance rendered by them in collecting material and critical reviews for this book. I would also like to express my gratitude to Ms. Evi Waldhauser and Ms. Sabine Jordan for the patient work that went into the preparation of the manuscript for this book.

1

Underdevelopment and its Causes

Does the North owe its development to the exploitation of the South, or is the South underdeveloped because of its social structures which hinder economic growth? The thesis that underdevelopment is the consequence of the South's incorporation into the capitalist world-system plays a pivotal role in justifying the demands made by the South of the West (comprising today's industrial market economies of North America, Western Europe and Japan). This forced integration commenced with the European voyages of discovery and conquests marking the fifteenth and sixteenth centuries. The following constitute the important stages of this integration:

— The conquest of the Latin America of today in the sixteenth century;
— The abduction of human labour from Africa through the transatlantic slave trade which, commencing in the sixteenth century, reached its peak in the eighteenth century;
— The take-over of the overseas trading routes in Asia and the exploitation of Asian societies by monopolistic European trading companies from the sixteenth century; the subsequent occupation of the most commercially relevant regions of Indonesia and India from the eighteenth century onwards;

— Discrimination against manufacturers from the Third World through monopolistic practices (and the use of armed force) until the eighteenth century and, through the principle of free trade adopted from the nineteenth century onwards, the effective 'deindustrialisation' of the countries of the South;

— The dismemberment of Asia and Africa by the colonial powers in the late nineteenth century, particularly from 1885 onwards;

— The specialisation of the Third World in the production of cheap raw materials (particularly from the beginning of the twentieth century);

— The role of 'multinational corporations' in the Third World with their monopolistic hold over the most advanced technologies (particularly since the Second World War).

In the context of this enforced integration, the South accuses the West of being responsible for its exploitation, of imposing on it an unequal specialisation and of being the cause of its economic and social 'deformation'.

Exploitation is the appropriation of value which is, consequently, no longer available for investment. This would explain the absence of economic growth through capital accumulation in the South. *Unequal specialisation* signifies that the West is favoured in commodity trade through its specialisation in technologically advanced products which are exported to the markets of the South. This, in turn, supports technical progress in the West, while manufacturing skills, which existed in the South even prior to the advent of the Europeans, dwindled or were destroyed by the Europeans perforce. In economic terms, *economic and social deformation* is said to come about when, as a result of exploitation and unequal specialisation, underdeveloped countries (here, the Third World) are deprived of those very avenues of production which are necessary for widespread economic growth; namely, the units for the production of capital goods which can generate employment and render the workforce more productive through new means of production. Without such units of production, growth depends on additional imports, which prove a burden on the balance of payment position. The countries of the South are socially deformed in the sense that extremely repressive political systems in the South were, and still are, supported by the European industrial nations.

with the aim of ensuring continued exploitation and unequal specialisation. Further, the creation of a historically progressive industrial bourgeoisie and a historically progressive working class was hindered; with the end result that, today, the process of bringing about changes in the social structure aimed at overcoming underdevelopment, stands obstructed. These accusations, which are adduced as explanations for the state of underdevelopment today, are supplemented by references to the inhuman repressive measures adopted by the European colonialists, who did not hesitate to indulge in economic warfare and genocide in their erstwhile colonies. In the eyes of the South, this long catalogue of iniquities is justification enough for it to demand from the Western industrialised countries that world income be redistributed in favour of the South since, according to it, the latter's poverty and underdevelopment was, and still continues to be, the consequence of the treatment it suffered at the hands of the North. The South further feels that the North had amassed the wealth it holds today on the basis of the exploitation, unequal specialisation and economic and social deformation of the South, and that it is rich and prosperous because it has fostered unequal conditions.

It is impossible to dismiss the list of iniquities which the South charges the North with. After all, the events presented as evidence are facts of history. The invasion of the Great Empires of the Aztecs and the Incas, spurred by the craving for gold, has become enshrined in the West's corpus of tales of daring and adventure. The colonial wars of the nineteenth century were fought with extreme brutality, for, here, the antiquated firearms and spears of the native peoples were pitted against the machine-guns of the colonists. The recruitment of the Red Indians as bonded labour and the transportation of approximately ten million Black Africans as slave labour to America, were carried out in terrible conditions. The peoples of the Third World were stripped of their cultural identity. Even though educated Europeans were, till 1880, aware that organised states with developed legal systems existed in subsaharan Africa, Africans were divested of their freedom and considered unfit to govern their own communities only twenty years later.

Nevertheless, even while conceding the fact of the West's discrimination against the South, it would still be dangerous to concur with the South in its conclusion that the West owes its development to the underdevelopment of the South. This is for the following two reasons:

1. If the economic development of the West rests purely on discrimination against the South, then underdevelopment can only be overcome through measures regulating foreign trade between the West and the South. (This is the 'inverse' flow of resources aimed at by the governments of the South, which will be dealt with in Chapter 4, while examining the demands of the Third World for a New International Economic Order.)
2. In attributing the development of the West to the inflow of resources from the South and the utilisation of the markets of the South, one overlooks the social structures in the West, through which labour was mobilised for economic growth. This also renders superfluous the question as to whether structural reforms within the social and economic systems of the South are necessary.

Consequently, as a first step, a substantiation is presented for the thesis that the exploitation, unequal specialisation, and economic and social deformation of the South did not constitute a precondition for the process of economic growth in the West, but were merely attendant phenomena. Indeed, the thesis contending that underdevelopment was caused by the incorporation of the South into the capitalist world-system is essentially self-contradictory. If the South had been exploited by the industrially developed countries of today, it must have been deprived of value (i.e., international purchasing power) which, consequently, could no longer have been available as export earnings for the purchase of imports. If a country is drained of value, it makes a bad customer for the goods which the industrial countries seek to supply it with in order to broaden their own export base.

THE EXPLOITATION OF THE THIRD WORLD AND ECONOMIC GROWTH IN THE NORTH: A HISTORICAL PERSPECTIVE

The primary economic motive behind European voyages of discovery since the fifteenth century was the quest for new sources of gold, or for direct access to the East Asian societies famed for their wealth. The objective was to reduce the balance of trade deficit of Western Europe vis-a-vis the Islamic countries of the Near and Middle East, where Europeans bought Indian, Indonesian and Chinese spices and cloth, especially in the Late Medieval Ages. The West European countries were unable to supply sufficient quantities of easily transportable, indigenously produced merchandise in exchange for these products. At the turn of the first millenium, for instance, slaves captured during the German colonisation of the East were supplied to the Islamic countries.

The Europeans concluded that they could only solve their balance of trade problem by either discovering new sources of gold, or by eliminating the Arab middlemen who controlled the land and sea-routes from the Middle East to India and on to the Moluccan Islands. Thus, the central objective of the European voyages of discovery was to discover a sea-route to India. This was met in 1498 through the discovery of the sea-route around the Cape of Good Hope. The European contribution to the discovery of sea-routes in the Old World was, for the most part, confined to the discovery of this route, since maritime routes from East Africa to India and Southeast and East Asia had already been discovered. After circumnavigating South Africa, Vasco de Gama took on board, in what is today known as Mozambique, an Arab maritime pilot who then guided him across the rest of the route to India.

The accidental discovery of the Caribbean and Central America by the Spaniards (Columbus in 1492), the discovery of Brazil (1500), and the step-by-step discovery of the North American continent by English, Dutch and French seafarers in particular, were merely by-products of the search for the route to India. These explorers were commissioned by their respective governments to discover new routes to East and South Asia, so that the sea-routes via Africa and Central America (from New Spain or Mexico to the Philippine Sea), which were controlled by the Portuguese and the Spanish until 1600, could be circumvented.

The discovery of the new sea-route to India across the Cape of Good Hope, and the other discoveries made in the process, especially in the New World, opened up the following opportunities for Europeans:

1. By gaining direct access to India, European seafaring nations (Spain and Portugal in the sixteenth century) assured

themselves of profits from overseas trade with South, Southeast and East Asia, profits which had hitherto been reaped by Arab merchant traders.

2. On the strength of their maritime supremacy (armed vessels), Europeans were able to gain control over even the intra-Asiatic maritime trade (for example, between India and Indonesia as also between Indonesia and China and Japan) and, in this manner, to secure additional commercial profits. While doing so, they eliminated any likely competition from Asian and Arab seafarers and restricted the possibilities of growth in trade and maritime activities in these regions.

3. Since the Dutch controlled the areas producing tropical spices from the seventeenth century onwards, cost of procuring these products could be reduced through coercive means.

4. The Europeans discovered new areas for mining gold and especially silver in Latin America and in some parts of Africa (for example, on the 'Gold Coast', Ghana and in the southern parts of East Africa).

5. In the Caribbean Islands, South America and the Brazil of today, the Europeans discovered areas of production in which spices and other tropical and subtropical agricultural products could be cultivated under their control.

6. The Europeans discovered rich cultures whose large stocks of gold and silver amassed over the centuries were open to plunder. In this regard, the Great Empires of the Aztecs and the Incas are well-known examples. Yet another example is the plundering of India after 1757, when the British East India Company came to exert direct or indirect control over large parts of India. The British began to collect state taxes which had previously gone into the coffers of local princes, an exercise which they carried out with 'greater efficiency'—in other words, with greater ruthlessness—than the previous rulers.

7. In Latin America, the Europeans 'discovered' the Indians, whom they put to use in different forms of bonded labour (*encomienda*, *repartimiento*, *mita*).

8. The Europeans also 'discovered' African peoples whose territories they had not occupied until the mid-nineteenth century (so far only trading settlements and forts had been

established, with the exception of the Cape Colony in South-West Africa), whose rulers were, nonetheless, ready to sell African labourers as slaves. These slaves could be put to work on landed estates in Latin America to raise tropical and subtropical agricultural products.

Given the above, the first wave (between the sixteenth and eighteenth centuries) of European invasions into the Third World had the following consequences:

1. The inflow of precious metals into Spain, at first predominantly from Latin America on the strength of working native Indians as bonded labour in the sixteenth and seventeenth centuries; subsequently from India, initially by looting the Indian princes and, later, by taxing Indian agriculture in the eighteenth, and even the nineteenth, century.
2. Cheaper production of tropical and subtropical agricultural products through bonded and slave labour.
3. Increase in profits due to the monopolistic organisation of the overseas trade of Asia, Africa and Latin America with Europe. Profits also accrued from the monopolistic organisation of maritime trade amongst these continents, as well as within South and East Asia.

   Initially, these profits went to the Portuguese and Spanish crowns which controlled these lucrative routes until the beginning of the seventeenth century. Subsequently, it was the Dutch who, for the most part, reaped the profits until their control over the routes was terminated by the English towards the end of the seventeenth and the beginning of the eighteenth century.
4. The highest profits were earned in the Atlantic slave trade: European slave-traders benefited from the monopoly prices fixed for agricultural products produced on American plantations, as well as from the low purchase costs of slaves, who were often exchanged for European manufactures of inferior quality, such as, pearls, iron rods, textiles, liquor, and arms. Even Brandenburg–Prussia was involved in this trade, though its influence was restricted.

The new possibilities of enrichment enumerated above were

undoubtedly based on exploitation. In the case of *forced labour* (as in Latin America and Indonesia), the indigenous people had to put in unpaid work in addition to working for their subsistence. The imposition of *poll* or *hut* taxes likewise compelled the local population to take up additional *unpaid* work, whereby the *earnings* again went towards taxes. The impoverishment of the indigenous peoples had serious consequences: This relentless recruitment as labour was one of the reasons for the decline in Mexico's population in the sixteenth century—from thirteen million in 1519 to two million in 1610. It is reported that in Indonesia, the indigenous population took to textile production as a cottage industry in the seventeenth century because they could no longer buy textiles previously imported from India.

The *slave trade* constitutes a particularly inhuman form of labour exploitation. Sizeable differences in prices for children and grown men (of about, the ratio 1:10), during the entire period marking the Atlantic slave trade, demonstrate that profits in slave trade, as practiced in the Modern Age, could be accounted for in the following manner:

The costs of capturing a slave were lower than the costs of raising a prospective labourer upto the age when he was fit for work. In order to acquire a workhand, a slave-owner had only to pay for the maintenance of the slave during the years he was fit to work, apart from the purchase and transport costs. The short life-span of slaves in the Caribbean Islands (about seven years) can be attributed to the fact that the slaveowners found it cheaper to pay as little as possible towards the maintenance of slaves, even if this meant that the latter were driven to their death within a short period of time. It was cheaper to buy new slaves than to increase the life-expectancy of the already acquired ones by curtailing the hours of work and providing better food. The costs of slave re-production, i.e., the costs involved in sustaining labour power over generations, were shifted on to African societies. The latter had to bear the costs of raising children *whom they could not, by virtue of the slave trade,* utilise as labour in their adult years.

The appropriation of monopolistic commercial profits amongst the continents of the South, and the looting of the princes and kings of Latin America and Asia also constitute the exploitation of today's Third World, because these profits—in the form of commodity money (precious metals)—had either been amassed earlier, or over a period of time. However, with respect to commercial profits earned from exports to Europe, both the societies of the South as well as European societies were exploited by trade monopolies. (In the case of the European societies this was due to the monopoly price at which these products were sold.) Especially in the case of goods which were not produced under European control, such as fine cloth (silk, cotton), porcelain, jade, spices (pepper, cinnamon, cloves, ginger), these trading companies commanded exorbitant prices from the European consumer, who was, generally, a member of those European upper classes who were not involved in overseas trade.

Some authors maintain that the various modes of exploitation mentioned above contributed to economic growth in Europe. According to them, *the inflow of precious metals* (especially from Latin America) led to a price revolution in sixteenth century Europe. To explain briefly, an increase in the supply of metallic money pushed up prices. As a result, those drawing high incomes stood to gain. These authors further hold that due to an increase in the 'profit mass', opportunities for investment financing (i.e., capital formation) also rose.

It is, of course, a well-known fact that this price revolution—to the extent to which it concerned the rise in price of foodstuffs in relation to monetary income—is attributable to the growth in population in sixteenth century Europe. Land which was less arable had to be utilised. Labour input for food production increased in relation to that for the production of precious metals and industrial goods. The inflow of precious metals could increase profits in real terms only if mass incomes or other incomes (for example, feudal rents) decreased, with the production level remaining constant. If only the supply of money were to increase, there would be an increase in the prices of all goods on par with the level of increase in money supply, the demand structure remaining constant. Entrepreneurs could, therefore, no longer purchase larger quantities of capital goods with the aim of making higher monetary profits, rather, they would have to pay higher prices for the same quantities.

The inflow of precious metals, however, had a different impact on different countries. Those parts of Europe into which precious metals flowed, principally Spain, revealed the strongest inflationary tendencies. Manufacturing production in Spain grew too expensive to withstand competition from other European countries.

Due to the inflow of precious metals, Spain threw open its markets to finished products from Northwest Europe in the sixteenth century.

The inflow of precious metals, therefore, only had the effect of redistributing competitive advantages in Europe, without generating funds for investment. Only the price of products requisite for economic growth registered an increase, on account of the new sources of monetary income, with there being no change in the real quantity of goods itself.

The concentration of money in the hands of the large overseas trading companies is viewed by some authors as a source of financing industrial growth in Europe. In reality, this money was often utilised to buy land, offices and, in some cases, to establish manufactories (for example, sugar refineries), but mostly it was used to finance wars. Industrial development in Europe started out with the expansion of small-scale production. These producers had always resisted the monopoly status of the trading companies. The purchase of land at high prices in eighteenth century England may be regarded as the sole contribution made by this concentration of monetary capital gained from monopolistic overseas trade. In this manner, members of the lower nobility and independent farmers secured starting capital for entering into industrial production.

The supply of *tropical and subtropical agricultural products* remained inconsequential for industrial development. These products can help to finance industrial development only if they either reduce the workers' cost of living, or the cost of capital goods. Until the close of the eighteenth century, Great Britain met sixty to seventy per cent of its statistically identifiable imports from the South, through coffee, cocoa, tea, and cotton (at that time only a small item), where, with the exception of tea (since the early seventeenth century), none of the other items constituted mass-consumption goods. Basic foodstuffs, and the principal raw materials of the Industrial Revolution, such as coal and iron, and even copper and tin, were produced in Europe, especially in Great Britain.

Only some dye-stuffs (Brazilian wood, betel nut, indigo), which constituted but a negligible proportion of the imports from the South, could be considered to contribute to the improvement in raw material supplies for the Industrial Revolution. This was true of dye-stuffs, since the dyeing of cloth constituted an important cost factor in the textile industry, which was one of the leading sectors of industrial development.

Thus, the sole *contribution of the Third World towards 'previous accumulation'*, i.e., the release of labour for the production of capital goods, before the breakthrough of the Industrial Revolution, lies in the fact that the supply of luxury goods from the South to the European upper classes meant that only a smaller proportion of European factors of production needed to be employed in the manufacture of such luxury items. The result was that this labour became available for the production of capital goods and mass-consumption goods.

This picture remains unchanged even during the *Age of Colonialism*, which is often looked upon as a period of *struggle for raw materials*. Following the establishment of raw material production in the colonies, the share of the South (colonies and independent countries, including Australia) in the total volume of world commodity exports still constituted 33 per cent in 1913 and 40 per cent in 1928. Minerals made up merely 16.3 per cent of African commodity exports, 13.2 per cent of Latin American commodity exports and 11.9 per cent of Asian commodity exports. It was only in the case of certain non-ferrous metals—initially, zinc, and then, copper—that the share of the Third World grew to be significant as early as in the 1930s. Oil exports from the Third World assumed importance only during the period between the two World Wars, while iron exports were sizeable only as late as in the sixties.

Economic growth in the industrial countries of the West cannot, therefore, be a consequence of the exploitation of the Third World. Rather, the concentration of wealth in the hands of trading companies served to reinforce monopolistic—bureaucratic tendencies, which, in turn, sought to restrict the market and competition-oriented production of goods. The inflow of precious metals did not signify a transfer of surplus value that was invested in production. By and large, the supply of cheap raw materials to Europe took place only in the twentieth century and had no bearings whatsoever on the breakthroughs that led to the Industrial Revolution.

THE MARKETS OF THE SOUTH: SUPPORTS FOR THE INDUSTRIAL DEVELOPMENT OF THE WEST

Until the end of the eighteenth century, all the European powers resorted to monopolistic practices to ensure markets for their own products. Even as early as the beginning of the sixteenth century, Portugal refused to comply with the request of the King of the Congo Empire in Central Africa for technical know-how in manufacturing. England banned the establishment of cities in some of her colonies with a view to preventing the emergence of centres of production. She further imposed production bans which, incidentally, were one of the causes for the revolt of the North American settler colonies. However, examples can also be advanced to counter this point. For example, from the sixteenth up to the eighteenth century, Spain supported the manufacturing production of its American colonies though admittedly because of the underdeveloped state of its own means of production. The British East India Company promoted textile production in India in the seventeenth and eighteenth centuries by securing external markets for it, and sought to improve production partly through the transfer of English know-how. From the mid-seventeenth century onwards, there were constant clashes between English textile manufacturers and the British East India Company over tariff policies relating to Indian textiles. To secure its influence, the British East India Company bought up members in both the political factions of the British Parliament with the profits reaped from monopolistic trading practices.

Production bans and measures for stepping up production are both equally a part of mercantilistic practices. It cannot be said that it was the nature of the West-South relationship that was the primary cause for the emergence of such practices, for these practices were in evidence within the West itself. The struggle for a balance of trade surplus and the appropriation of specie made manufacturing a sector through the expansion of which those countries which were not endowed with large resources of internationally tradable raw materials were most likely to gain additional revenue. From the Middle Ages up to the eighteenth century, German cities sought to ban manufacturing in the surrounding villages. Mercantilistic states banned the import of those industrial goods from other European countries which could be locally produced, and sought to bolster the export of manufactures, partly through providing subsidies. Moreover, industrial production in the Third World was encouraged where it served the interests of the mercantilistic nations, in that it provided substitutes for imports from other regions (from England in the case of the Spanish colonies in Latin America); or, in that additional exports (from India into other countries) contributed to an increase in monetary reserves.

However, viewed in quantitative terms, these mercantilistic practices were of consequence neither for the South nor for the West. In England, the leading industrial nation of the time, between 1690 and 1798, the export quota fluctuated around 10 per cent, betraying a slight tendency to increase. However, the major proportion of these exports did not go to what constitute the countries of the South today. In fact, the oft-advanced contention that the volume of manufactured products exported to the South in the eighteenth century underwent a rapid growth is based on erroneous statistical definitions. For instance, the decline of Spain in the eighteenth century and, as a consequence, its monopoly over trade with the Spanish colonies allowed an increased volume of British goods to be directly supplied to Latin America, without having to pass through Spanish ports. To be sure, the proportion of overseas markets receiving English exports (inclusive of Spain and Portugal) did increase from 47 per cent at the beginning of the eighteenth century to 74 per cent at the end of the eighteenth century, but it was the market of the North American settler colonies, and not that of the South, which registered the most substantial increase (from 6 per cent to 41 per cent). The proportion of English exports marketed in what is today's underdeveloped world, therefore, rose only from 41 per cent to 43 per cent. It should be noted that in the eighteenth century, amongst what constitute the industrialised countries of today, England was the nation that was oriented towards the markets of the South.

At the beginning of the nineteenth century, there existed manufacturing centres (of textiles, among others) all over the Third World. In fact, India's textile production had to be kept out of the English market through protective tariffs even up to the beginning of the nineteenth century. Similarly, despite every effort made by England to gain access to the Chinese market (for example, through the despatch of a trade mission in 1792), China, to a considerable extent, remained closed to European exporters of manufactured goods until 1840. There was no demand for European finished products in China; Chinese tea exports were paid for not with manufactured products but with opium. The Anglo-Chinese

War (known as the Opium War) of 1840–42 was triggered off by the Chinese ban on the sale of opium. Thus, the South had no notable markets to offer for the products of the West, at least not in the period prior to the Industrial Revolution in England.

Nevertheless, this does not counter the allegation that the competitive advantages gained by Europe over the South on the strength of its technical achievements—characterised by the Industrial Revolution—led to the stifling of manufacturing activities in the Third World in the nineteenth century (following the advent of the Industrial Revolution in Europe). This was evidenced when Great Britain opened up the markets under the pretext of free trade, by partly employing military force.

Whether the opening up of the South's markets promoted industrialisation in the West is a question which has to be answered on the basis of the share of the South in exports from the newly industrialising countries of Europe and North America. Only in the case of England did the South grow to be an important market in the second half of the nineteenth century (and even here due to the imports of the Latin American Republics), when the process of the colonial dismemberment of the world began. The new colonies in Africa, on the other hand, were relatively insignificant. Only the smallest proportion of Germany's and the USA's exports went to the South (see Table 1). In the last third of the nineteenth century, these two countries 'caught up' with England and France on the industrial front, and grew into leading industrial countries by virtue of their development in new branches (chemicals and electronics).

The South's contribution to the technical advancement of the industrialising countries was even less significant than its quantitative share in the exports of the North. Enterprises introduce new technologies as a process innovation with the objective of reducing production costs. Rises in the cost of labour, and of raw materials in particular, promote this type of innovation. A fall in the prices of raw materials and the availability of cheap labour in the Third World can hinder this form of technical progress.

A prerequisite for technical progress, when viewed as product innovation, is expanding mass markets, for new products can only be mass-produced if there exists a wide market offering ample marketing avenues. New products and new production techniques are developed in economies in which the highest mass incomes; at

TABLE 1

Percentage Share of the South (A) and of the Colonies (B) in the Exports of Important Industrial Countries (1860–1910)

	USA	Great Britain		Germany		France	
	A	A	B	A	B	A	B
1860	4.8	33.3	20.7	n.a.	n.a.	n.a.	n.a.
1870	1.1	34.5[1]	16.7[1]	n.a.	n.a.	16.1[1]	5.1[2]
1880	11.7	41.7	16.3	n.a.	n.a.	20.6	6.3
1890	13.2	45.5	18.2	n.a.	n.a.	21.2[3]	7.1[3]
1900	14.5	31.6	15.9	12.0	0.4[4]	21.1[5]	12.6[5]
1910	19.4	43.1	6.1	13.7	0.5	22.0	13.6[6]

Sources: Statistical Yearbooks of the countries concerned, various issues.
N.B. The South = the rest of the world excluding Europe, USA, Canada, Australia, and New Zealand.

[1] 1875.
[2] Only for Algeria in 1875.
[3] 1889.
[4] Only for German East Africa.
[5] 1899.
[6] Algeria constituted half of France's external market in its colonies. This can be accounted for by the demand among the European settlers for industrial products.

any given time, create a widespread demand for new goods and a strong compulsion to reduce labour costs through labour-saving techniques. It is, therefore, not surprising that new industries emerging at a particular period of time have their principal markets in the most developed economies. Thus, it was more the 'older' industries (such as textiles or, for that matter, the distilling industry), and not the developing industries of the time, which were interested in the colonisation of the countries of the South. The fact that colonially protected markets for established industries hindered structural changes in France and Great Britain towards the end of the nineteenth century, partly explains why these countries later fell behind the USA and Germany.

The insignificant role played by the markets of the South in the industrial development of the West does not, however, rule out a consideration of the claim that the exports of finished products from the West in the nineteenth century wrecked the manufacturing production of the South. The opening up of Egypt (1838–1840) and the stifling of the Indian textile industry are widely quoted examples in support of this thesis. In Egypt, the reformer Mohammed Ali attempted, from 1821 onwards, to 'catch up' with Europe on the industrial front through state enterprises. The monopoly on the Egyptian market enjoyed by these enterprises was arbitrarily brought to an end by Great Britain in 1842, thereby bringing about the decline of these enterprises. At the beginning of the nineteenth century, India met as much as 96.1 per cent of its textile requirements from its own production; in 1880–81 this figure had sunk to 41.6 per cent, with local production declining from 361 million lbs. to 250 million lbs. Further, it can be shown that in Latin America, competition from European manufactured exports led to the decline of the most advanced and favourably located centres of manufacturing production, especially from the mid-nineteenth century onwards.

Such evidence of the decline of manufacturing production in the Third World, as brought out in several studies, should, however, be further explored. English goods were competitive in Third World markets because they were cheap. The era of free trade witnessed a uniform deterioration in the relationship between the prices of manufactured exports from England and the prices of primary commodities from the Third World. The competitive suppression of manufacturing production in the Third World through price undercutting was, therefore, linked to an improvement in the terms of trade (the relationship between the import and export prices) of the South. Furthermore, the examples cited do not even hint at the complexity of the observable processes of deindustrialisation of the Third World. Competition from Europe did not initially affect manufacturing production for the masses; rather, it was production for the higher income groups that was affected in the first place. The decline in the production of Indian handicrafts as early as in the eighteenth century was not the outcome of the growth in European exports but of a fall in the incomes of the Indian princely and elite classes. This was the result of the British East India Company having arrogated the right to collect land tax, consequent to its having taken over large sections of the country after 1757.

Complex processes of simultaneous deindustrialisation and the growth of manufacturing production can be observed in both India and China in the nineteenth century. In both countries, the import of cheap English yarn paved the way for the growth of a small-scale weaving industry, particularly in the rural areas. Everywhere in the Third World, this small-scale rural industry withstood the pressures of the era of colonialism and free trade, even though widespread poverty impaired its potential for growth. Even in the urban areas, free trade led to industrial growth in the Third World. As early as around 1880, textile factories were established in India which, by the turn of the century, were displacing English textile exports in East Asian markets.

Contrary to the oft-advanced contention, the principle of free trade was neither completely absolute in its application, nor was it entirely imposed from outside. The chief buyers of European goods in the nineteenth century were the Latin American countries and not the colonial dependencies, not even China, whose markets were forced open at the point of a gun and through the so-called 'unequal treaties'. The majority of the Latin American countries introduced high tariffs, at the very latest by 1890 as was the case with Brazil. These tariffs served as protectionist barriers behind which individual branches of industry, such as the textile sector, grew rapidly. Even though England applied pressure on the Latin American countries, as in the nineteenth century, the tariff policy adopted reflected an internal clash of interests: Primary producers and exporters—for the most part native-born —were interested in free trade and asserted themselves against other social groups.

Hence, in conceding that the development of manufacturing production in the nineteenth century was impeded by the 'imperialism of free trade', one should not overlook vested interests within the Third World itself which encouraged the enforcement of free trade.

RAW MATERIAL WEALTH–RENT–UNEQUAL SPECIALISATION

Due to their natural wealth, countries with rich raw material reserves constantly face the threat of being forced into a situation of unequal specialisation while trading with countries which are not so richly endowed. Given equal labour costs and the same level of technical development, a country with greater raw material wealth can produce raw materials at a cheaper cost than a country with fewer natural resources. By specialising in commodity production, a country with raw material wealth can, for the same amount of resources employed, import a greater quantity of finished products from its export earnings than it can produce locally. Raw material wealth renders capital investment in commodity sectors more remunerative than in the manufacturing industry. Consequently, there is no incentive to develop manufacturing production.

This tendency is further strengthened by the modes of price formation peculiar to primary commodities. Since the natural conditions of production vary according to individual regions and deposit beds, often within a particular country itself, the costs of production for the very same raw materials also vary accordingly. However, a uniform market price is fixed on the world market. Producers with favourable natural conditions of production, therefore, draw revenue which is higher than the costs incurred. The difference between revenue and production costs (including average profit for capital invested) is termed differential rent.

On the basis of technical innovation, a capitalist entrepreneur engaged in manufacturing may realise a higher rate of profit than the average rate of the national economy concerned. This above-average profit should be reinvested by him under conditions of free competition, since his competitors are 'catching up' on the technological front. Given a sufficient level of total demand, profits from the manufacturing industry, even so-called extra profits, should be utilised for further capital accumulation. Differential rents emerge on the basis of existing natural conditions. These conditions continue to prevail if the differential rent is not invested.

Thus, raw material production generates income which need not necessarily be utilised for technical advancement. Often, the concentration of natural resources in the hands of individual landowners gives rise to a situation where differential rent accrues to only a few in the primary exporting country concerned. As a result, income distribution becomes extremely inegalitarian because, among other reasons, the recipients of rent tend to buy up available assets. Where the distribution of income is extremely uneven, markets for manufactured products are small.

Even if such rents are not clearly discernible, they can still hinder the development of manufacturing production in an indirect way. The historical process of development reveals that capital productivity during the initial stages of industrial development tends to be low (partly due to high infrastructural costs), then gradually increases to reach a point of stability. Profit rates in the developed industrial countries are, therefore, on an average higher than those in the Third World.

Capital from the West is invested in the Third World only if the profit rate expected here is as high as that in the industrial countries. This applies only to some sectors, and primarily to commodity production. Under this condition, the profit rate in certain sectors of the lesser developed country is higher than the average profit rate in the same country, although on an average it is comparable to that in the more developed country. Profits from the commodity sector of the less developed country can, therefore, only be invested in a few branches of indigenous production which are allied to the commodity sector (for example, some luxury-goods producing industries). If such a country were to devalue its currency, then local factors of production would become cheaper by international standards. The costs of production of goods hitherto imported would fall in relation to the world price. Commodity production would also become cheaper. Since commodity production was competitive even at the old exchange rate, the country concerned could levy export taxes without in any way impairing the acquisition of average profits.

Average profits are, therefore, generated in commodity production when the national currency concerned possesses an external value at which it appears to be more cost-effective to import manufactured products rather than produce them locally.

Good commodity prices prove to be disincentives for the diversification of production. Countries with poor natural resources should, on the other hand, improve their manufacturing production through investments in order to pay for their imports. In this way, they can also develop new technologies and products. *The presence of raw material wealth did not hamper development in only such countries as in which high incomes from primary exports led to the formation of a broad-based mass market, thanks to either a wide distribution of land holdings, or to other social mechanisms.* Furthermore, pressure of competition from foreign products was restricted in such countries through tariffs, or as a result of natural barriers (transport costs). This is true of areas settled by the Europeans (the United States, Australia, Canada, New Zealand), and of Northern Europe (Norway, Denmark, Sweden, Finland):

though even in these areas, migration to the United States and living conditions in the mid-west during the second half of the nineteenth century were important factors for the costs of labour, and hence, for the structure of demand itself.

Industrial development in the Third World was not hampered by exploitation but by the relative wealth of the Third World itself. Even if the Third World had not been exploited and no force had been employed to open up markets, the willingness to enter into free trade, following the advent of the Industrial Revolution in the West would at first, have necessarily led to the deindustrialisation of the South, unless income from commodity export was so well distributed among the mass of the population so as to create a broad-based domestic market for mass-consumption goods.

THE FOUNDATION OF GROWTH OF INDUSTRIALISED CAPITALIST COUNTRIES

We have seen how the contribution of today's Third World to capital accumulation through the supply of cheap raw materials and foodstuffs was almost insignificant. The same holds true for providing markets for industrial goods in what constitutes the South of today. Both misconceptions could not possibly have arisen had leading 'bourgeois' and Marxian theories not maintained that the basis of the Industrial Revolution of the West was primarily capital accumulation. This, in turn, forms the basis of the argument that the South could overcome underdevelopment only through increased investment, which is to be mobilised either through greater exploitation of the population, or through a transfer of resources from the West. To discount this, a brief discussion is required, concerning the genesis of capitalism and on the Industrial Revolution in the West. This discussion serves to substantiate the thesis that, apart from investment, industrial development requires the expansion of mass consumption.

Industrial production is characterised by the use of machinery which is run on non-human energy. Machinery differs from tools in that it is employed to execute identical and constantly recurring (repetitive) operations. A woodworking machine always treats identical pieces of wood in the same manner. With a tool, on the other hand, a piece of wood can be worked into a variety of forms.

Machines can be employed where products of the same type are required to be produced in large quantities. The utilisation of machinery will be profitable if many consumers demand products of the same type. The existence of a wide mass market is, therefore, a prerequisite for industrial production. At a given level of aggregate income in an economy, the size of the mass market is larger where the income distribution is more even. Profits can be accumulated to form industrial capital only if the methods of production involving the employment of machinery prove to be remunerative or, in other words, if mass markets exist. For, accumulation is not merely the amassing of wealth but also its investment in new machinery.

New production techniques are remunerative only when they succeed in reducing unit costs. A reduction in unit costs can, for the most part, only be effected by curtailing the number of working hours required to be employed for every unit of quantity produced. Here, 'direct' labour can be supplanted by 'indirect' labour represented by the machine. The total volume of work invested in production employing a new technology decreases when calculated in terms of the life of the machinery. Therefore, real wages remaining constant, aggregate wages decrease when a new technology is introduced. To be sure, the 'capitalists' can, for a short while, offset this fall in demand through increased investment. These investments, however, invariably create additional capacities in proportion to the labour input. This is why technical progress achieved at stagnating levels of real wages quickly gives rise to excess capacities in relation to mass demand. Similarly, capitalists cannot offset the fall in demand through increased personal consumption since the pressures of competition compel them to reduce prices at par with cost reduction. Technical progress in industry requires not merely mass markets but *growing* mass markets.

This thesis runs counter to the widespread belief that the lower classes were reduced to poverty during the initial stages of capitalistic and industrial development in Europe. In this connection it is contended that:

— A mass of the poor lived below the poverty line and were compelled to take to industrial labour as proletarians.
— The chief promoters of industrialisation were big, capital-owning entrepreneurs.

— The real income of the industrial workers was low and underwent a decline during the Industrial Revolution.

Let us start with the problem of compulsory labour for the poor. The *Poor Laws* introduced in England, at the close of the sixteenth century, enjoined the parishes to provide a minimum subsistence to the poor, in return for which the latter were committed and compelled to work (provided they were fit). These laws envisaged drastic sanctions for those unwilling to work, but, as we know today, they remained to a large extent unimplemented. There existed at that time a large number of exemptions, as, for instance, the possibility of staving off such sanctions by invoking the Bible. Viewed in economic terms, these *Poor Laws* did not constitute a form of exploitation, but rather a redistribution of income in favour of the masses.

It goes without saying that the English parishes could not have fed the poor without taxing the rich. The rich drew their incomes from property holdings created by the surplus product of the gainfully employed workforce. Such income would not have been generated had the rich not engaged labour on their estates. The imposition of taxes served to reduce the income of the rich and further subsidised the poor. The parishes could then offer these poor people to entrepreneurs or landowners as wage labour, at wage rates below the subsistence level. Since the subsidies were financed from tax collections, they could not possibly exceed the amount already raised by way of tax from the rich. Labour whose productivity was low cost the entrepreneurs less than the subsistence costs of this labour. The reason for this was that labour was partly financed by taxes paid by the entrepreneurs and the landowners themselves out of profits gained from the employment of labour whose productivity was higher than its wages. Viewed in economic terms, this means that labour whose marginal product was lower than its subsistence cost was financed by taxes on profits accruing from the employment of labour whose marginal product was higher than its cost of maintenance.

In a less developed economy with low average productivity of labour, the work performed by one additional labourer may lead to an increase in production which, however, is lower than the cost of providing this worker with the minimum subsistence, although total production is high enough to provide for all the workers. A

few labourers combined with the few available means of production yield high profits, whereas the employment of all the labourers
only results in declining profits. Entrepreneurs cannot maximise
their profits if they employ every available workhand If profits
gained from production with few workers were to be taxed, then
the community procures financial resources against a loss in
'profit'. In this manner, the difference between the means of subsistence requisite for those not hitherto employed and the production increase achieved by these workers on their being employed
will be neutralised.

The Poor Laws of England constituted an effective instrument
to fight unemployment at the expense of profits gained, and served
in the interest of an expansion in mass incomes, since the additional workers employed produced an additional output that was
less than what they consumed. The Poor Laws prevented marginalisation as is generally discernible in the South today. A policy
measure corresponding to that of the Poor Laws for the South
today would lie in taxing entrepreneurs and big landlords heavily
in order to finance a programme to feed the marginalised who, in
return would, be required to work in industrial enterprises for low
wages.

The *expulsion of the rural folk* by enclosing what had hitherto
been utilised as community land—as referred to mostly in connection with Thomas Morus' sixteenth century indictment: 'Sheep
would graze on men'—did not take place in the manner depicted
in popular scientific literature, which often draws on Marx. In the
sixteenth century, enclosures were restricted by the so-called
Population Acts. The English Crown, which was impoverished at
that time, needed independent farmers who could be recruited as
members of the militia, since it could not afford a standing army. It
was only in the eighteenth century that there was a mass move
towards enclosures, a move occasioned by the rising demand for
foodstuffs, and not by the expansion of the low labour-intensive
production of wool for export.

Since the discrepancy between the rich and the poor is smaller in
the case of food consumption than in the case of other items of
consumption, we may look upon the rise in productivity, particularly for foodstuffs, in the English agricultural sector—often
characterised as the Agrarian Revolution, which occurred, at the
very latest, from the mid-seventeenth century onwards—as indicative

of the fact that the poor in England, unlike the poor in today's Third World, were able to ensure that they did not face death through starvation. Compared to the Continent, the food situation of the mass of the population was more favourable in seventeenth and eighteenth century England. In England, the improvement in food production was linked with highly labour-intensive investments in agriculture, particularly in soil improvement, so much so that there was no decline in the number of jobs available in the agricultural sector until the first third of the nineteenth century.

To be sure, there was an increased concentration of landholdings in England in the eighteenth century. However, this was not brought about by a forcible eviction of the peasants. High profits from overseas trade were utilised by commercial capitalists for making safe 'investments' in land. The price of land rose. The gentry and the independent farmers sold their land and invested the proceeds in the more profitable manufacturing production. During this period, the investment need per person employed in agriculture was nine times that of the manufacturing sector.

Hence, it was not the big commercial capitalists engaged in overseas trade who were the chief promoters of the Industrial Revolution. Rather, the Industrial Revolution in England was preceded by a phase marking *the rapid development of small enterprises*, a phase in which the lower nobility and former peasants expanded manufacturing production in areas where no guilds existed.

It was not the manufactories—for the most part unremunerative large-scale enterprises—which financed the consumption of the members of the absolutist ruling state apparatuses through monopolies, but rather these small-scale enterprises themselves. These formed the mainstay of the growth of manufacturing production, right up to the Industrial Revolution. Parallels to the small-scale sector in the South, which, today, is once again receiving more attention, and to the inefficient functioning of public enterprises in the Third World, are but obvious.

If England witnessed a rapid growth of employment in small industries and agriculture, besides experiencing the mechanism of redistribution in favour of the poor, then the contention that there was a *decline in real wages* at the start of capitalist development is hardly plausible. This thesis is often justified on the basis of the index of wages drawn by construction workers in London, which is, however, hardly representative. The findings of more recent research in England actually go to show that the wages of labour increased in real terms as early as in 1760–80, and again in 1820 and, therefore, not as late as, as is claimed, the mid-nineteenth century. It has been shown that the Industrial Revolution gained a firm foothold in the Midlands, a high–wage district of England with a small concentration of landholdings, where there was an increase in real mass consumption. Many people from other parts of England migrated to the area at the end of the eighteenth century and the beginning of the nineteenth century, because of the better employment opportunities there.

High labour incomes, and relatively egalitarian structures of distribution can also be detected even in the case of countries which were successful 'latecomers' to industrialisation, particularly the USA. Both Argentina and Australia exported similar primary commodities for a long time. Considering this, the difference in their respective development paths can only be explained by the existence of a relatively egalitarian income distribution in Australia, as compared to Argentina.

HISTORICAL IMPEDIMENTS TO DEVELOPMENT IN THE SOUTH

In the fifteenth and sixteenth centuries, the South had societies which were more egalitarian than those of Western Europe; however, these existed only in those areas where the mastery of Nature, in other words, technology, was still in its initial stage of development. The rulers could appropriate only a small surplus product. One would assume that where there is nothing to be had, there is accordingly nothing to be distributed, as a result of which, differences in income are but small. Yet, even the majority of the *African societies* which can be cited as examples here, were well on their way to developing marked social disparities, even prior to the advent of the Europeans. Growing intra-African foreign trade permitted the rulers, who controlled trading routes with the backing of their well-developed armies, to acquire commercial profits through trade monopolies. In order to strengthen their control over these routes on which their incomes depended, these rulers expanded their military apparatuses. Consequently, there emerged a class of warriors who also assumed administrative functions. Many

African Empires, such as Ghana or Songhay in the West, the kingdom of the Congo in Central Africa, and Zimbabwe in East Africa, emerged in this manner through external trade.

Although such kingdoms bore similarities to the feudal systems of Europe, they distinguished themselves from the latter through certain important characteristics: These African kingdoms did not know of any institutionalised conflict amongst the elite—as between followers of the Emperor and the Pope in Europe—and neither did they have land possession rights which were protected against the power of the 'state' (the sovereign), as did the feudal lords against the princes of Europe. Furthermore, since the ruling class was not segmented into relatively independent landowners, as in Europe, these kingdoms did not experience the emergence of independent cities which attempted to attain independence by playing off one lord against another.

Hence, we should regard Third World societies which appear to be relatively egalitarian as disintegrating 'communal modes of production' whose social differentiation lead to the emergence of a centralised ruling class. This is, however, only prototypical of the second main type of society that the Europeans came across during their expansion into the Third World: the tributary mode of production, which also goes by the names of 'oriental despotism' and 'Asiatic mode of production' (since it was first examined in relation to India, China, Turkey and Persia).

The *tributary mode of production* is characterised by the appropriation of a substantial portion of society's surplus product by a centralised State–class ('functionaries', soldiers). Membership to this class is on the basis of office. The State–class' share of the society's surplus product is determined on the basis of the status of individual members in the official hierarchy. The appropriation and distribution of the surplus product takes place on the basis of state authority. In some societies, the state assumes certain functions in the economy, minimally, functions such as stocking, which guarantee it ready access to the surplus product. In certain other societies the state maintains the irrigation works.

Since no member of this State–class can increase his personal income substantially in the long run, either through technical innovation, or by motivating the workers (for the most part farmers) under his control, technical innovation will not provoke any enduring interest. China knew of many innovations earlier than

Europe. However, it was seldom that the Chinese showed an interest in applying these innovations. This 'incidentality' of technical progress is attributable to two development tendencies of tributary modes of production which are complementary to each other; namely, the tendency towards increased consumption of luxury goods, and that towards the restriction of competition in the manufacturing sector.

A 'dynastic' cycle has been described thus by Ibn Khaldun for the Arab world, and by the Chinese historians for their Middle Kingdom: At the beginning a dynasty is still weak (as with the African ruling classes). Gradually, its power, which is rooted in military strength and religious authority (the Chinese Emperor is regarded as the Son of Heaven), increases and with that its capacity to collect taxes. There is a growing concentration of consumption within a small upper class. While the per capita income in India during the reign of Elizabeth I of England is estimated to have been as high as that in England, reports of travellers of the sixteenth and seventeenth centuries all concurrently state that the standard of living of the Indian farmer was far below that of his British counterpart. In contrast, practically all European travel accounts up to the end of the eighteenth century wonderingly draw attention to the opulent life style of the Indian upper classes as far more luxurious than that of the British elite.

The concentration of consumption within a small privileged class gives rise to three divisions within the small trade sector. First, there are centres of production which are spatially bound to the sites of mineral wealth (for example, salt), and are controlled by state trading monopolies (in the case of salt, this can be evidenced in almost all the great civilisations of Asia). Together with these, there is, on the one hand, a village crafts industry which stagnates due to low mass incomes (as opposed to a dynamic rural manufacturing production in Western Europe), and on the other, an urban crafts industry which is oriented to upper class consumption. It is this urban crafts industry which is referred to when the high level of development of manufacturing production in the ancient empires of the Aztecs and the Incas, or in India, China and Egypt is extolled. This manufacturing industry deals with the production of luxury goods: the customers in this case are not interested in cheap products but in products of excellence.

Technological progress does not primarily aim at reducing the number of working hours invested per unit of output but at the production of individual pieces of increasing excellence. There is only negligible interest in employment and hence, in the development of machinery itself. At the same time, this primary orientation towards product quality strengthens the monopolistic tendency inherent in guild-based trade. Often, the state even concentrates manufacturing production in state workshops. Tributary modes of production, therefore, have comparative advantages in the production of luxury goods vis-a-vis the European feudalistic setup, due to the thrust and direction of their technological progress. This is, however, not the case with the production of mass-consumption goods.

The above mentioned cyclic movement from a lesser to a greater degree of exploitation, to which the peasants react by fleeing, curtailing production, or rebelling (if lesser quantities are produced, the state responds by increasing the rate of taxation), does not effect a fundamental change in these societies. All such resistance movements lead to the establishment of a new dynasty which, in its turn, once again adopts the course of increased consumption and exploitation. The stagnation of these ancient empires is accounted for neither by the claim that peasants were tied to the village communities which prohibited them from holding private property, nor by the contention of the absence of market relations. As a matter of fact, this picture of the Indian village community was invented by the English tax authorities in India, who considered collective taxation of entire villages more efficacious than the individual taxation of farmers on the basis of their family incomes.

In many tributary modes of production, farmers were the *de facto* owners of their land even though all land was, formally speaking, state property. In all these empires, there were extensive commodity–money relations or, in other words, trade. Yet, what proved to be the main impediment to the transition into a capitalist economy and society was the establishment of a centralistic State–class as the enduring dominant authority. Moreover, the persisting low standards of living of the masses did not permit the emergence of a social class capable of pursuing its own material objectives by investing in machinery for the manufacture of mass consumer goods, under conditions of market competition.

The transition from a communal to a tributary mode of production typifies the standard case in history: the transition to European feudalism, on the other hand, the exception. At a relatively high level of development of the forces of production (in all times recorded by history, even in antiquity), strong forces opposed the recentralisation of the elite to form a State–class and succeeded in aborting the attempt, at least in eighteenth century England. European absolutism represents the ultimate efforts in this direction. Denied this recentralisation, the feudal lords saw themselves compelled to accept the existence of rival centres of power in urban areas and thus, sought to try to enhance their incomes by interesting the farmers in production and productivity increases in material terms, for by merely stepping up exploitation they would have forced the farmers to migrate to the cities. In fact, the adage 'city air liberates' ('*Stadtluft macht frei*') applies only to Western Europe.

THE DEFORMATION OF THE THIRD WORLD THROUGH CONTACT WITH RISING CAPITALISM IN THE NORTH

While the contact between the West and the South did have a positive effect on growth–impeding structures in the Third World, it did not, however, lead to the emergence of the mechanism of rising mass incomes and industrial accumulation, characteristic of the capitalist industrial countries, in the South. Such a mechanism would have promoted the development of technology for the low-cost production of standardised goods.

In *Africa*, social differences favouring the emergence of tributary modes of production increased: Without mobilising the masses, individual societies armed themselves in revolt against the European incursions. African slave-hunting monarchies and bridgeheads of external trade with the Europeans emerged with European cooperation, in the seventeenth and eighteenth centuries.

In *Latin America*, the colonists took over the rights of the indigenous classes to tribute and gratuitous work. Although these rights of exploitation of Indian labour were taken over by private individuals (through Crown grants), this did not necessarily signify that European feudalism, which was relatively open to competition and to resistance from the lower classes, was being transported to

Latin America. Instead, what emerged here was an extremely repressive system of exploitation which, following centuries of conflict between the Spanish Crown and the colonists, ultimately led to the establishment of a society with extremely inegalitarian land distribution. This, in turn, served as the basis for the formal, or the *de facto*, imposition of forced labour. Attempts at liberalisation, during the Wars of Independence of the early nineteenth century, were successfully crushed by big indigenous landlords and traders. These classes merged together to form relatively coherent oligarchies.

In *Asia*, ruling State-classes did initially try to ward off European incursion through greater centralisation and the adoption of European military techniques. However, the possibility of high profits through contact with the Europeans quickly resulted in the decline of centralisation. This is often characterised as the process of feudalisation. Tax-collection rights, vested in the office, were transferred into land ownership rights, partly in response to the demand of European colonial powers (as in India), thereby resulting in greater concentration of land ownership. Further impetus was given to this process by the export of raw materials.

We can, therefore, speak of a *convergence of underdeveloped countries* to form an inegalitarian type of society, controlled by small oligarchies comprising of big landlords, exporters and government officials (to a certain extent under colonial rule). Greater concentration of land-holdings combined with the simultaneous disintegration of the rulers' commitment towards the lower classes—a consequence of the principle of profit maximisation supplanting old bonds of solidarity—destroyed even that minimum of social security which pre-capitalistic social structures had conceded.

A factor common to all Third World societies is the non-transference of basic elements of the bourgeois value systems. Where the privileged classes of the Western industrial countries are concerned, the striving for wealth and the enforced, and constantly jeopardised, acceptance of competition have become constitutive of their society since the rise of capitalism. In the countries of the Third World, competition is less of an accepted norm.

The lower classes in the bourgeois societies of the West are associated with the values of solidarity, equality, liberty, the right to a certain level of material prosperity, the demand for reform in case of grievances, and the value of social equilibrium. These values of power curtailment and conflict negotiation were not transmitted to the Third World. Nor was it ever the intention of the Europeans to transmit such values to the Third World. In order to reduce the costs of administration, the European powers backed the authority of those members of the ruling class who were willing to cooperate with them, thereby contributing to the repressiveness of the local political systems, if they actually did not create such inhuman political systems themselves. A case in point is the system of so-called direct administration in colonial Africa and parts of Asia.

The West transmitted neither its socio-economic nor its political system to the South. The South was not totally capitalised, rather, it integrated itself into a system of unequal specialisation either freely of its own accord, or under duress. In this system of unequal specialisation, the material wealth of the privileged depended not on growing domestic mass markets but on export to the industrial countries of the North. The idea of a bourgeois revolution was, likewise, forbidden by the North to the South. To cite an example, the French Revolution (1789), in its first phase, consciously sustained slavery in the French colonies. Thus, the revolution in Haiti led to the establishment of the first free republic in the South only at the beginning of the nineteenth century.

When such markedly inegalitarian societies came into contact with capitalistic industrialising societies, the following processes resulted: In the developing societies of the West, there was along-term increase in real wages, at par with the average growth in labour productivity. Consequently, prices of goods from branches with a below-average growth in labour productivity had to necessarily rise in proportion with the overall average price of goods. In the nineteenth century, since raw material production faced the problem of technical progress being counteracted by the depletion of cost-effective deposit beds—for it is always the well-known, low-cost beds which are worked first—the prices of raw materials rose in relation to the prices of manufactured products.

At the same time, rising mass incomes also created new mass needs, as for instance, tropical agricultural products. Due to the low level of industrial development, the cost-effective raw material sites of the Third World had not yet been worked. Besides, tropical agricultural products could only be produced in the South. In the short term, the South's specialisation in mineral and agricultural raw materials is consistent with the distribution of comparative cost advantages. This pattern of specialisation only served to further aggravate inequality within the framework of social structures in which the underprivileged were unable to induce gradualistic changes in income and power distribution to their advantage. Markets for mass-consumption goods emerged only in very limited sectors of primary-exporting countries, for example, as in the case of essential commodities for subsistence living.

Without an expansion in mass production, there was a lack of incentive to develop local capital goods production. A broad class of skilled labour was not created in the metal-working sector, which is necessary for the emergence of this class. An economy is inflexible when it lacks the capacity for indigenous capital goods production. An economy is said to be flexible when a change in the relative prices of goods, for example, a decline in export prices in relation to import prices, gives rise to processes of adjustment. Export production becomes less profitable, goods hitherto imported grow dearer, local producers become more competitive and consequently, expand production. Production expansion in branches oriented to the domestic market calls for a rapid increase in capital investment, or, in other words, the investment of additional capital goods.

A country which is incapable of producing at least a part of its capital goods requirement will not be able to expand production even with such a change in relative prices. This is due to the fact that new investments will only increase the volume of imports which have become more expensive for the underdeveloped country, owing to the fall in export prices in relation to import prices. This, however, does not imply that developed countries must meet their entire capital goods requirement themselves. It only means that the level of technical development in these countries enables them to meet increased demand even for hitherto imported capital goods, by virtue of the fact that they can enter into such production without high start-up costs.

This mechanism works because total factor productivities in different branches are adjusted continuously through the reshuffling of the system of relative prices. In a capitalist text-book economy, additional output per additional factor quantity invested (labour, capital) tends to be equal in every employment when measured against the price: If labour in an expanding branch A were to secure a higher additional output than in branch B, on the basis of high demand and good prices, then the entrepreneurs of branch A would be ready to draw additional labour away from branch B by offering higher wages. The same is true of capital flows. Here, it is however assumed that differences in the additional production of goods per total factors employed (measured in prices), i.e., total factor productivity, do not vary greatly from branch to branch.

It is the absence of this condition that distinguishes underdeveloped countries from developing and developed ones. Productivity is generally high in export sectors and in some sectors producing luxury goods for the rich; it is, however, low in sectors oriented to mass consumption. In most Third World countries, the proportion of labour employed in agriculture is generally twice as high as the contribution of agriculture to the gross national product (measured in product prices). The labour–productivity lag vis-a-vis the industrial countries is especially high in the case of technology production, though lower for the labour-intensive production of consumer goods, especially for assembly-line production. Where there are wide divergences in factor productivities according to the branches of production, price increases in the wake of increases in demand or changes in import prices are often too small to stimulate production in the branches concerned, since capital still does not realise an average profit rate owing to low factor productivity.

The inflexibility of Third World economies is revealed by the branch-to-branch divergences in total factor productivity. It is this condition, termed 'structural heterogeneity' (and not the coexistency of divergent modes of production), which constitutes the structural characteristic of underdeveloped societies. It is the outcome of the transfer of the system of relative prices from the West to the South. To a large extent, it rules out flexible adjustment to a changing demand, with the effect that it becomes difficult to bring about gradual changes in income distribution and effect reforms. Potentials of social conflict are intensified, rather than mitigated. The structure of production contributes to the merely incomplete transfer of the reformist aspects of the Western system of norms.

In sum, structural heterogeneity is the result of the absence of local technology production. If technology could be produced indigenously, it would be possible to equip local productive capacities with machinery which need not be paid for in foreign exchange but whose production on the other hand, would generate employment. Even if the South were to protect its industries from the world market, the beginning of production in new branches would, in most countries of the South, be dependent on the import of Western technology (due to the product quality demands of the rich and the lack of technical skills in the production of capital goods).

Structural heterogeneity, therefore, intensifies because the South whose production is not oriented to a growing mass demand fails to utilise the domestic mass market as leverage for the development for local technical skills. Structural heterogeneity can only be overcome through complex strategies which reproduce the growth mechanism of mass consumption–accumulation–technological development through the planned restructuring of production and social structural reforms.

2

The Social Structures in The Underdeveloped World: Their Impact on North–South Relations

THE IMPOVERISHMENT OF THE THIRD WORLD

The tangible economic and social outcome of the partial integration of Third World countries into the capitalist world-system lies primarily in poverty and dependence. According to World Bank estimates, 780 million people lived below the poverty line in 1975, of which half were from South Asia, mainly from India and Bangladesh. A further one-sixth hailed from East and Southeast Asia (making a total of two-thirds from Asia) and a sixth from Black Africa. These people mostly lived in rural areas. The World Bank reports that—although comprehensive data on poverty are lacking—since 1980 the situation has taken a turn for the worse as economic growth rates have fallen, real wages have dropped, and the growth-rate of employment has faltered in most developing countries. Precipitous declines in commodity prices have cut rural incomes and governments have reduced their spending on social services. Table 2 gives some poverty indicators for Third World countries.

These countries are classified into the following specific groups by the World Bank: Developing countries with low incomes (GNP per capita upto $ 425), countries of the middle-income group

TABLE 2

Poverty Indicators for the Third World, by Country Group

	GNP per Capita: 1980	Annual Average Growth Rate of GNP Per Capita (1965–86)	Per Capita Food Consumption	Population Per Physician: 1970	Primary School Enrollment in % of Age Group	Infant Mortality (in the 1st year)		Life Expectancy at Birth: 1986
						1965	1985	
	($)	(%)	(calories)			(0/000)	(0/000)	(No. of years)
Low-income countries	270	3.1	2329	6050	97	127	72	61
Low-income countries (excl. India and China)	200	0.5	2100	17670	70	150	112	52
Middle-income countries	1270	2.5	2719	4940	104	104	68	63
—lower middle-income countries	750	2.8	2511	7880	103	132	82	59
—upper middle-income countries	1890	2.5	2967	1340	105	84	52	67
Oil exporters	930	2.5	2664	7020	93	140	88	59
Exporters of products	540	4.0	2483	2340	106	87	56	64
Highly indebted countries	1400	2.3	2607	4580	104	107	66	63
Sub-saharan Africa	370	0.9	2097	25310	77	167	104	50
Oil exporters with high incomes	6740	1.8	3213	1380	75	115	61	64
Industrial market economies	12960	2.3	3357	550	102	23	9	76
Non-reporting countries	n.a.*	n.a.	3304	300	105	33	32	69

Sources : Statistics from World Bank and UN Agencies.

N.B : n.a. = not available.

* : only Kuwait.

(GNP per capita above $ 425), which are further divided into lower middle-income economies and upper middle-income economies (GNP per capita above 1800 $). The latter group is, however, rather heterogeneous and includes the newly industrialising countries of Argentina, Brazil, Hongkong, Korea, Singapore (52 per cent of the population of the group); seven oil exporting countries (Algeria, Gabon, Iran, Iraq, Oman, Trinidad and Tobago, Venezuela, 19 per cent); some East European countries (Poland, Hungary, Romania, Yugoslavia, 16 per cent); and Greece, Israel and Portugal (4 per cent). Within the group of middle-income countries, the World Bank distinguishes between oil exporters (which do not comprise of the high-income oil exporters such as Kuwait, Libya, Saudi Arabia, United Arab Emirates), exporters of products, highly indebted countries, and subsaharan Africa. These subgroups tend to overlap. It must be noted, however, that even if we exclude from consideration the high-income oil exporting countries whose GNP per capita includes the high (rent) incomes from oil exports, differences between the various groups of countries remain considerable.

Low-income countries with a total population of 2.49 billion (1986) can be further classified into three groups: the People's Republic of China with a population of 1054 million, India with a population of 781 million, and the rest of the countries with a combined population of 658 million. With the exclusion of China, the low-income group of countries fares worse than the middle-income countries with regard to the poverty indicators specified in the table.

Gradually, however, the middle-income countries are catching up with the industrialised countries of the West, even in the area of per capita production. In 1986, 1.28 billion people lived in these countries, of whom 730 million resided in oil importing countries. These countries had registered the highest GNP growth rate between 1960 and 1986 (4.01 per cent). The average GNP of these countries was five times as high as that of the low-income countries in 1980 and in 1986, although for some members, oil revenue had declined. This difference, expressed as a percentage of the incomes of other countries in 1980, was as high as the figure by which this group lagged behind fully developed countries such as Great Britain, although this distance had increased in 1986 to 7:1. This group of middle-income countries also recorded an improvement in the living conditions of the poor, at least in terms of the child mortality rate. The calorie intake per head is adequate and a greater section of the population benefits from public services, for instance water supply and primary education.

A closer look at the individual countries, however, reveals that the eradication of poverty does not depend on the GNP level. Within this group of middle-income countries itself, there are wide differences: Infant mortality in South Korea is three times as high as that in the industrialised countries drawn into comparison, though it is only a sixth of that in Burkina Fasso, one of the poorest regions of the world. In 1980 and 1986, it was only half as high as the level of infant mortality in Brazil, whose GNP per capita in 1980 was 25 per cent higher than that of Korea, and in 1985, 25 per cent lower, with the per capita food supply, however, being consistently lower than that of Korea.

To be sure, there are extremely poor countries who register poor values for many indicators but especially in the case of the middle-income countries, there is no clear connection between poverty and national income. Population per physician in India (3700) and China (1730) is less than half the average of the lower middle-income countries, although GNP per capita is only about one-third. Furthermore, infant mortality in India has come down, and is now at a level slightly higher than that in the lower middle-income countries. In 1965 China's rate had declined to below that of Spain. Oil-rich countries such as Oman, Iran, Nigeria or Indonesia have less favourable indicators than India. Life expectancy in the upper middle-income economies is slightly above the level achieved in India and China.

This brings us to the problem of income distribution as an indicator of accessibility to economic goods. This indicator should be relativised to the extent that, particularly in poor countries, poverty control and the satisfaction of basic needs rest on the spread of infrastructure and public amenities, such as medical care. The extremely impoverished countries are characterised by a relatively egalitarian income distribution (with 40 per cent to 50 per cent of the income drawn by the highest 20 per cent. and 6 to 10 per cent by the lowest 20 per cent); however, the middle-income countries reveal wide disparities. Here, for the most part, 50-66 per cent of the income goes to the highest 20 per cent, and a mere 2–3 per cent to the lowest 20 per cent. However, rapidly developing countries like Singapore, Hong Kong, Korea and Taiwan reveal relatively egalitarian structures—as compared to other middle-income countries—with 5–9 per cent of their incomes going to the lowest 20 per cent of the population, and 40–45 per cent to the highest 20 per cent. These structures of distribution can be compared to the distribution of income in the more egalitarian of the West's industrialised countries.

Thus, although poverty, in absolute terms does exist in many countries of the Third World, disparities within the middle-income group give no room for the expectation that economic growth by itself can eradicate poverty.

POVERTY AND THE STRUCTURE OF PRODUCTION

A fact of central importance to the issue of poverty is the low productivity of agriculture. In 1980, 71 per cent of the population in the low-income countries (as against 77 per cent in 1960), and 47 per cent of the population in the oil-importing countries of the middle-income group (as against 65 per cent in 1960), lived off agriculture. In the low-income countries, the contribution of this section of the population to the GNP amounted to 50 per cent in 1960, 36 per cent in 1980 and 32 per cent in 1986. This shows that productivity of agricultural labour measured against productivity of labour in the remaining sectors declined from 64 per cent in 1960 to 51 per cent in 1980 and 44 per cent in 1986. In the oil-importing, middle-income countries, the contribution of agriculture to the GNP declined from 28 per cent in 1960 to 14 per cent in 1980 and to 12 per cent in 1986. Accordingly, the relative productivity of agricultural labour measured against the productivity of the rest of the economy also fell from 43 per cent in 1960 to 30 per cent in 1980. The neglect of agriculture in many oil-producing countries is a widely documented phenomenon.

The problem of poverty in the Third World, therefore, goes hand in hand with the problem of a neglected agricultural sector. The yield per hectare for wheat and rice (in quintals) is 14.4 and 18.1, respectively, in Africa; 22.8 and 33.1 in Asia, and 19.1 and 21.5 in Latin America, as compared to 42.3 and 52.9 for Europe, and 31.9 and 61.9 for Japan. During the last decade yields increased in the Third World by 5 to 20 per cent. Without an increase in food production, and, therefore, necessarily in the yield per hectare, poverty control is not possible in the long run; for, when the income of the poor rises, they will, first of all, demand more food.

The growth of industry, whose share of employment between 1960 and 1980 rose from 10 per cent to 15 per cent in low-income countries, and from 16 per cent to 22 per cent in oil-importing, middle-income countries cannot, by itself, solve the poverty problem, considering the fact that industry in the Third World offers just under forty million jobs for a growing population, whose unemployed are at present estimated at about 350 million. But without poverty eradication, it is not possible to stem the rise in population. As long as children remain the only source of social security and make vital contributions to the family income, population control programmes can only have a long-term effect if mass poverty in the Third World decreases.

Statistically corroborated successes in industrialisation should be viewed with some reserve: Although the contribution of industry to the GNP rose from 32 per cent to 37 per cent between 1960 and 1980 in the oil-importing countries of the Third World, the share of the manufacturing industry stagnated. Moderate increases can be observed in China and India and some Asian countries which have entered export-oriented industrialisation, whereas we observe stagnation in the import-substituting countries of Latin America. In countries with rapidly rising shares of production, such as South Korea, gross output rose in 1980-85 by 8.3 per cent, whereas productivity rose by 9 per cent. Gross output per employee in India rose by 5 per cent (1980-85), total production by 4.8 per cent. Employment, therefore, could not increase. In the highly indebted countries, the share of manufacturing production even decreased between 1980 and 1986.

Success in efforts at industrialisation seems to be most apparent in the sphere of expansion of the basic industries and not in the diversification of industrial production, with the exception of the export-oriented industrialising countries. At the same time, on the supply side, the process of industrialisation in the developing countries has led to an increasing dependence on the industrialised countries, for, with the exception of countries like China, India, Brazil, Mexico, Argentina, South Korea and Taiwan, the developing countries have not built up their own capital goods industry.

Despite this trend, there has, however. been a certain development: In 1971, 13.6 per cent of the total diesel motor production came from the Third World (excluding China); in 1979 this figure had risen to 19.4 per cent (489,000), of which India accounted for 57 per cent, and the leading Latin American countries for 29 per cent and in 1986, this figure stood at 304,000 or 15.3 per cent. In the case of agricultural implements, the Third World's share of world production amounted to 0.5 per cent in 1971, 12.8 per cent in 1979, and 14.6 per cent in 1985. Between 1970 and 1978, the capital goods imports of the developing countries rose from $ 20 billion to $ 54.5 billion at 1970 prices, their local capital goods production from $ 10 billion to $ 20 billion, subsequently appearing to stagnate until 1985.

The share of the Third World in world production of non-electrical machinery rose from 3.2 per cent in 1965 to 4.8 per cent in 1975, but declined to 4.3 per cent in 1985. The share in electrical machinery (including consumer durables such as TV sets and refrigerators as well as transport equipment), rose from 5.4 per cent (5.3 per cent) to 7.1 per cent (7.5 per cent) and to 7.0 per cent (7.7 per cent) in the respective years. Hence, there was less of an increase in technological independence and more of a delocalisation of the production of consumer durables to the Third World. The production of the four major metal-working machines (grinding and sharpening machines, lathes. milling machines, other metal cutting machine tools) amounted to 310 million units in 1980 (world: 968 million), and 368 million units in 1985 (world: 806 million).

In 1980, corresponding imports of machinery and transport equipment amounted to $ 149 billion, and to $ 148 billion in 1986 (in prices of 1970, 63 and 53 billion). Imports from Non-OPEC countries had increased from a nominal value of $ 64 billion in 1978 (total of all developing countries: $ 104 billion) to $ 97 billion in 1980 and 115 billion in 1986 (in prices of 1970 this was $ 51 billion in 1978, $ 41 billion in 1980. and $ 34 billion in 1986). On the basis of OECD export statistics, only an estimated fourth (1986) of this class of goods which qualify as producer goods (SITC 71 to 74), whereas this share was still about one-third in 1980.

THE NEW SOCIAL STRUCTURES OF THE THIRD WORLD

The penetration of capitalism into Third World societies, the presence of Western colonial administrations and the participation of Western enterprises in the Third World economy, coupled with the international 'demonstration effect' gave rise to new social structures and new expectations in the South. Both these developments had an even greater impact on the attitude adopted by the governments of the South towards the North than the actual pauperisation of wide sections of the population in the Third World. Special emphasis should be placed on the developments discussed below.

The Transformation of the Feudal Land Owners into Agrarian Capitalists

While analysing the deformation of the Third World through its contact with the North, the disintegration of traditional bonds of solidarity between the ruling classes and the peasants has already been focused upon. This process was the outcome of new possibilities—open to the privileged—for securing profits and for utilising such profits for consumer goods imported from the West. This process has accelerated since the Second World War, as a result of social and technological factors. As a reaction to the Chinese Revolution, the governments of the Third World recognised the agrarian issue as one of central importance for the maintenance of political stability. They were effectively supported in these efforts by the USA.

In 1950, the first set of plans for land reform was introduced for international discussion. Agrarian reform was an important aspect of the programme drawn up for the 'Alliance for Progress' which President Kennedy concluded with the Latin American states in 1961. The crux of the analysis of Third World agrarian structures lay in the contention that the big feudal landlords dominant in these parts were neither willing nor in a position to use their land efficiently and step up production. In fact, various studies have, in particular, established that the yield per hectare was inversely proportionate to the acreage under cultivation.

The outcome of this analysis was the legislation of laws for agrarian reform providing for the expropriation of unutilised land. One of the most important strategies for circumventing these laws lay in the shift-over to modern agrarian technologies and the weakening of tenancy rights with the objective of rendering baseless the demand that land should belong to the people who work it. Short-term leases and the shift-over to mechanised production brought about a decline in the number of tenants who could benefit from this principle.

Although some countries of the Third World (Mexico, India, Chile, Peru, Egypt, Iraq, Iran) did witness some measure of land redistribution, the power of the landed aristocracy remained intact in most of the countries. Wherever land came to be redistributed (outside of China, Vietnam and Cuba), the governments concerned oriented themselves to viable medium-sized holdings, i.e., to holdings of a size which, due to the poor availability of agricultural land outside Latin America and Africa, made land inaccessible for a good section of the rural population. Due to the understandable predilection of the middle farmers for engaging their own labour and family hands on their newly acquired estates, the landless sections of the rural population were worse off than before the redistribution when they were at least engaged as seasonal labour by the big landowners.

The availability of new methods of production based on new seeds (hybrid varieties), intermediate chemical inputs and mechanisation accelerated the process of rationalisation and the trend of growing unemployment in agriculture. It must be said of most of the intermediate inputs utilised while applying new production technologies that there are no technological barriers to their employment. Even small farmers can employ them on their plots. But since these intermediate inputs push up extraneous costs, on the one hand, and increase the agricultural surplus product, on the other, such technologies have generally favoured producers with large financial reserves and bigger plots. Despite the oft-contended positive side-effects on employment in the field of repairs, the new technologies destroyed job opportunities for rural labour because, with only a limited expansion of markets, the effects of rationalisation were felt all the more: For a production output which was only marginally greater, the new technologies required a smaller indigenous labour-force, both direct and indirect.

The Emergence of the Middle Farmer

Alongside the generalisation of capitalist relations of production in agriculture on the basis of the transformation of the landed aristocracy, there emerged a class of market-oriented middle farmers. Both the introduction of limited agrarian reform and the disintegration of communal modes of production on land served as a basis for the emergence of this class, a class which still reveals sharp disparities on the basis of capital goods and land endowment.

The process of the development of communal modes of production into societies of middle farmers had begun on the African continent by the end of the nineteenth century. Following the establishment of colonial systems in Africa from 1884 onwards, it soon became clear that the plantation system was not competitive in the production of exportable cash crops. This was due to two factors operating on smallholder farming: On the one hand, the political costs of effecting large-scale expropriations of land proved to be too high in relation to the economic gains, at least for the foreign colonial powers (although not necessarily for the 'national' elite, as has been proved in the case of Firestone in independent Liberia in the 1920s). On the other hand, small and middle farmers in Africa, and even farmers in Malaysia and Indonesia, were able to produce agricultural exportables at less cost than the plantation owners, the reasons for this being the increased employment of family hands as labour for reasons of economy, the compulsion to cultivate the land as a result of the introduction of poll taxes, or the access to cheap labour.

The market-orientation of a section of the peasantry in the Third World led to the disintegration of the communal system of land cultivation. Private ownership of land emerged, which, coupled with the concentration of land holdings, led to the creation of a class of middle farmers. This class grew more prominent in countries with limited agrarian reforms. Such middle farmers produce marketable surpluses and are dependent on world prices and the official pricing policy for intermediate inputs and agricultural produce. Often, they were the forces behind political movements protesting against a decline in world prices, or against a state pricing policy too strongly oriented to the interests of the urban population.

Industrial Labour in the Third World

The integration of the Third World into the capitalist world-system not only hindered processes of industrialisation but, paradoxically, also induced them. Such processes of industrialisation developed even within the context of free trade, for example, through the expansion of local markets subsequent to the growth in commodity exports. Since labour incomes in the Third World were far below those in the industrialised countries, individual branches of production in Third World countries became competitive vis-a-vis the industrialised countries, despite registering low rates of labour productivity. The Indian textile industry of the late nineteenth century is a case in point.

Some processes of industrialisation owed their development to the suppression of small-scale local production by local industrial production with imported technology, partly shielded by protectionist barriers. Protective tariffs, introduced even before 1914 in some of the formally independent countries of the South, were in greater evidence in the 1920s, even, as a matter of fact, in the areas under colonial rule (India, mandated territories in the Middle East).

These tariffs also found universal application during the world economic recession of the thirties due to the fall in export opportunities for primary commodities. This, consequently, introduced processes supplanting hitherto imported goods through local products, with these processes being intensified in many Third World countries as a result of the Second World War, for the Western countries at war had only a limited capacity to supply goods due to the war effort. The mobilisation of resources in the backward regions of the Allied countries of the West to finance the war fought in the Middle East and East Asia also led to the growth of industrial production in these regions. With the attainment of political independence (1945–48 in Asia, 1960–63 in Africa) by countries which had hitherto been under colonial rule, the national governments of these countries could regulate their external trade, which they generally used as a means to promote the development and expansion of national industries.

To be sure, these different processes of industrialisation did not generate full employment in the countries of the South. What emerged was a local, urban class of workers, whose role has become the subject of conflicting standpoints. A sizeable section of authors is of the opinion that this class of workers is the force spearheading socio-revolutionary movements. Due to their social status as proletarians, these workers—as contended by this group of authors—are characterised by a level of consciousness which differs qualitatively from that of the peasants. This different consciousness gives the workers the capacity to act as a class on behalf of all the other lower classes in order to surmount the exploitation perpetrated by the imperialistic practices of the capitalist industrialised countries and the local ruling classes.

Undoubtedly, workers in the modern, large-scale enterprises of the Third World did, and still do, represent a potential of resistance. Strikes directed against foreign domination and deplorable living conditions were organised even at an early stage. Every now and then it can be observed, at least in the case of Africa, that the impact of the social movements of the urban proletariat spilled over to the rural population as well. In practically every colonial dominion, workers' organisations (trade unions) and nationalist parties with a proletarian support base constituted important centres of organisation for the rise of liberation movements.

On the other hand, workers in modern large-scale industries constitute but minorities in all Third World countries. Their potential ability to organise themselves poses a threat to political stability. For this reason, Third World countries are inclined to meet the demands of organised trade unions, at least their major aspects, and to accommodate them in the political decision-making process. At the same time, these workers possess a certain level of skill, as compared to the mass of the unemployed. The industrial concerns of the modern sector in the South—be they public enterprises, MNC–affiliates, or local private enterprises—employ modern technology. Greater fluctuation in the availability of semi-skilled labour brings about a greater increase in costs, than would result if wages paid to these workers were high in relation to the general level of income.

Furthermore, labour costs, in the case of capital-intensive modes of production are less of a consideration than capital costs in the case of a shutdown in production. In an attempt to stabilise the availability of skilled labour, ward off social protests that impair day-to-day operational runs, and in view of the scarcity of skilled labour itself, all Third World enterprises of the modern sector tend to pay relatively high wages. Direct wages and indirect services, as for example, from the state social-security systems, provide the workers of the large-scale sector with certain privileges, irrespective of their status of ownership.

For these reasons, many writers see in the workers of the Third World modern sector a privileged class which, to a certain extent, might even be willing to defend the interests of MNC–affiliates, where these happen to be their employers. The different social movements of the Third World suggest that the proletariat of the South conducts itself in a fashion akin to the reformist tendencies of its counterpart in the North. Anarcho-syndicalistic tendencies often mark the beginning of their class struggles. Subsequently, the workers cease striving for a durable change in the prevailing social structure and, instead, aim at an improvement in their economic situation. The international 'demonstration effect', i.e., the desire to attain the level of consumption prevailing in the industrial countries, contributes to the emergence of such a primarily income-oriented strategy in the Labour Movements of the Third World.

It is often maintained that such an orientation prevents the development of bonds of solidarity between the workers and the mass of the underprivileged, namely, the rural population, since the real incomes of urban labour are, to a large extent, determined by the prices of basic foodstuffs. Practically all Third World governments have set up marketing boards which enjoy a relatively strong position as buyers of agricultural produce from the farmers. Apart from these boards providing their personnel with an opportunity to amass wealth, often through corrupt means, they also serve the objective of keeping the prices of foodstuffs low for the urban population.

Producers in the Small-Scale Sector

Not everyone employed in sectors other than agriculture finds employment in the modern sector of industry. In the fifties and sixties, there was an ongoing discussion on the role of small and medium-scale enterprises in the Third World. Since the early seventies (World Employment Programme of the ILO 1969), this broad-based and often rapidly developing sector has, once again, been receiving particular attention as the 'informal sector'. Up to seventy per cent of the manufacturing production in individual countries is accounted for by one-man undertakings, family concerns, or small-scale units employing less than ten workers, none of which stand to gain from the State Industrial Promotional Schemes. This sector draws from the traditional skills of artisans, enhances the workers' level of qualification through training (apprenticeships), and engages in a labour-intensive mode of production using local technology and local inputs.

The sector also depends on the growth of the modern sector and agriculture. From the perspective of employment opportunities, the informal sector emerges due to the limited absorptive capacity of the large-scale sector, established with the help of imported modern technology, the release of labour in agriculture, and the growth in population. Rural labour migrates to urban centres in the hope of securing employment in the modern urban sector (even outside of industry, as for example, in the administrative or service sectors), for, even long periods of waiting in the city afford economically attractive prospects. If a person, by working in a modern industrial concern, were to earn a real income at least six times of what he earns as a rural labourer, he would be willing to wait a few years for a steady job.

These observations explain the large-scale migration from the land and the growth of urban centres in all Third World countries. In 1950, 40.8 per cent of Latin America's population lived in cities; for Africa the figure was 14.8 per cent, for East Asia, 16.8 per cent, and for South Asia 16.2 per cent. Corresponding figures for 1980 were 65.4 per cent, 23.8 per cent, 32.7 per cent, and 24.8 per cent, respectively. Figures projected by the UN in 1982, for the year 2025, are 83.6 per cent, 58.6 per cent, 62.3 per cent and 55.8 per cent. It will be noted that in the cities, the informal sector of small and infant enterprises offer an initial, and what is often regarded as a temporary, source of employment. This sector also happens to enjoy marketing avenues for its products and services for a variety of reasons: the rich spend a considerable portion of their incomes on traditional services, whose growth does not contribute to economic progress.

However, in the case of the manufacturing section of the informal sector, the principal market for these products is constituted by the urban and rural poor. For these poorer sections, the cheap low quality products turned out by the informal sector provide them their only opportunity to satisfy the compelling need for manufactured products. Soap or furniture constitute very different products in the Third World, depending on the income of the consumers. Price differences for goods of the same intrinsic value (excluding top quality luxury goods) are in the range of approximately 1:2 in the Western industrialised countries, whereas the ratio for Third World countries is 1:5 (for example, sandals in Nigeria).

Despite frequent discrimination by the official development policy, the informal sector has ultimately stood to gain by official development efforts, especially by the development of a modern industrial sector, for, due to these efforts, new markets have been thrown open to it. Often, incomes paid in the modern industrial sector are higher than the production achieved, with the effect that there is an increased demand for goods from the informal sector. Bottle-neck situations in repair activity are often eliminated by the informal sector. Thus, repairs, textiles, building construction and furniture constitute the main branches of specialisation of the growing number of goods-producing small and infant enterprises.

The 'National' Bourgeoisie

The informal sector appears to be more important, in terms of potential for economic development, than the 'national' bourgeoisie, which is often regarded to be a force that counters excessive dependence on the West, but is also equally often criticised as being a 'compradour bourgeoisie'.

The term 'compradour bourgeoisie' initially included wholesale merchants who were involved in the functioning of all local levels in the West–South trade. Such social groups rose quickly within the framework of West–South relations—for instance, the emergence of merchant princes on the West African coast, as early as in the seventeenth century. The rise of this class is attributable to the fact that the final marketing of European products and the purchase of local products from the producers were, in general, not undertaken by the European import-export houses. In the twentieth century, the term was also applied to industrialists who employed Western technology in their production, and who were, even if minimally, dependent on supplies from the West, but who, today, are also dependent on the Western industrial countries for their markets.

Others, however, see in this class a national bourgeoisie, because of its differences with foreign suppliers and buyers, and particularly because of its efforts to close the domestic market concerned to foreign competitors by adopting certain protectionist measures.

This dispute about the characterisation of this bourgeoisie is, in fact, quite futile, for this bourgeoisie is not in a position to reorient the domestic markets to rising mass incomes and, in this manner, to create the growth mechanism of 'profitability through the expansion of mass consumption.' In periods of an adverse foreign exchange position, this class will tend to depend more on the national market; alternatively, during periods marked by a favourable foreign exchange position, it will turn to international co-operation. The mere fact that they are poorly represented in most Third World countries and maintain close links with the local landed aristocracy, which often takes to such manufacturing activities, rules out the contention advanced by Stalinist development theorists and Western proponents of the theory of modernisation, that this bourgeoisie could play the historically progressive role of the bourgeoisie in the industrial countries of the West.

The 'New Middle Class

The 'new middle class' of the Third World comprises of those educated in modern 'Western' schools who, however, do not own any means of production themselves. Viewed in a broad perspective, these new middle classes can be characterised as the 'intelligentsia' a term which is often assigned the epithet 'national'. The vigorous rise of these classes in the twentieth century, particularly during the late colonial phase in Asia and Africa, and since the world economic recession of the thirties in the politically independent countries of the South, is the outcome of complex processes.

In an attempt to reduce their costs of administration, the colonial governments decided to venture into the training of indigenous personnel. To do so, they established some schools, which came to be the only sources of western education. Labouring under feelings of inferiority vis-a-vis the West, the local elite sent their children to such schools. In the context of late-colonial development programmes, the colonial powers accorded top priority to the expansion of the educational system because it was assumed that the primary cause for underdevelopment, expressed in terms of low labour productivity, was the lack of education. The same is true of official development efforts of independent Latin American countries since the thirties, and of Africa and Asia at a later period, in accordance with their respective developments.

The fact that colonial and independent governments accorded special importance to secondary and collegiate education only goes to show how successful the 'elite' of the West were in securing recognition for their misconceived notion that it was the elite, and not the skilled workers, who were the mainstay of economic growth. This new middle class is most evident among the liberal professions (doctors, chemists, advocates, notaries), followed by professions of the establishment, such as the civil administration and the army. The members of the new middle class seldom become entrepreneurs. This was because they lacked the requisite capital and markets for setting up large enterprises. Small-scale enterprises were not an attraction as they yield lower incomes and lower prestige than the public sector and the liberal professions. However, if the members of the middle class were to gain access to monetary capital through corrupt means, they would have, perhaps, financed such enterprises without, however, getting actively involved in them.

Since a section of those with Western education did not, and still do not, find avenues for employment, and since this class is, at the same time, most vulnerable to the international demonstration effect (due to the very nature of its education), it often provides the recruitment ground for forces of socio-revolutionary and anti-imperialist counter-movements. These forces adopt Western elements with the objective of modifying their own culture, where they often advance the argument of restoring the original nature and vitality of their respective cultures. However, despite differences in weightage accorded these two elements (adoption of Western elements, revival of traditional elements), these forces constitute the mainstay of the process of a partial and oft-interrupted Westernisation.

NATION-BUILDING IN THE THIRD WORLD

Nations owe their emergence to the disintegration of traditional systems and to the resulting social movements. Problems can no longer be solved within the narrow confines of the regional context. Social groups organise themselves within the framework of larger units (states) and set up institutions to resolve mutual conflicts. This process is facilitated by a shared historical, ethnic and cultural heritage.

The concept of the nation in the modern sense of the word presupposes that the lower classes participate in the political process, at least to the extent that their demands are accommodated by the rulers in the event of social change, even if this change is a paternalistic decree from above. In the theory of politico-social modernisation, nation-building in terms of a greater integration of the society concerned becomes the objective of political development and a precondition for economic growth.

Nation-building in the Third World has to contend with social anomie, sharp social class differences and segmentations. Anomie is to be understood as social disorganisation caused by the break-up of traditional social ties, without the creation of new social structures to replace them. *Segmentation* is the vertical splitting up of people living together on one territorial unit—the state. Segments generally comprise of people from all social classes and are distinguished from other segments on the basis of characteristics which are not class-specific, such as ethnic affinities (to small ethnic groups, which are then referred to as a 'people'), religious affiliations and regional particularisms.

Since growth processes are restricted in the South to only 'islands of economic progress', so-called poles of development, are formed. Growth impulses existing around them, in the form of demand for labour and manufactured goods, are generally too weak to effect a long-term increase in the level of economic development. Regional conflicts of interest within the developing countries themselves are, therefore, extremely pronounced.

Religious segmentation plays an insignificant role in Latin America and in the Confucianist cultural milieus of East Asia. But, as opposed to this, the Hindu–Muslim divide on the Indian subcontinent during independence (1947) led to one of the largest migrations of peoples known in history (15.3 million refugees). Even today, conflicts between different religious groups play a significant role in India's internal politics. In the world of Islam— which extends along the traditional trading routes of the Old

World between Western Europe, Black Africa, India (here, along the valleys of the Indus and the Ganga), beyond the Moluccan Straits to South Philippines, and along the ancient overland silk route upto Western China—there are numerous examples of clashes between sects and brotherhoods (for instance, in Lebanon). The Islamic Revolution in Iran and its implications for important Arab States of the Persian Gulf has drawn the West's attention to the Shiite–Sunni divide.

As a consequence of traditional rivalry between Christianity and Islam, two missionary religions, it was extremely difficult for the Islamic countries to synthesise modernisation in the political, economic and social fields with the preservation of their own cultural identity. This is especially so because in Islam—as initially in other religions as well—there is no bifurcation between the spiritual and the temporal spheres. This factor has grown to be an important component of the process of cultural identification directed against the West. Thus, in the Islamic world, segmentation also takes place between partially Westernised groups and Islamic fundamentalist groups. In Black Africa, Christianity, introduced by the colonists, local religions, and Islam confront each other, as also in Nigeria, with the Christian Ibos and the Muslims in the Northern States opposing each other (the Biafra conflict, 1967–1970).

Viewed from the ethno-linguistic perspective, not all the ancient empires with tributary modes of production now form homogeneous nations. If the problem of ethnolinguistic diversity in the Arab World can still be regarded as a problem concerning individual ethnic minorities (the Berbers in North Africa, the Kurds in Northern Iraq), this cannot be said of the South in the Old World where—with the exception of Korea, China (which, however, has minorities in the South and the East), Vietnam (with the hill peoples as minorities), Iran (with national minorities), Turkey (again, with national minorities), and Somalia—no state is made up of one national group. In Latin America, the Western observer gets the impression of ethnically and linguistically homogeneous societies, but in reality, individual Latin American countries have powerful non-Hispanised Indian minorities concentrated in certain regions, who are frequently subjected to racial discrimination.

Segmentation need not, however, hinder the formation of a nation, as is demonstrated in the case of biconfessional Germany or multilingual Switzerland. However, in societies with a low level of economic prosperity, segmentation can lead to the hegemony of certain social segments over especially lucrative sources of wealth. These groups subsequently preserve these economic advantages for their own members. For the members of different segments who, however, share identical social and economic status, social and economic discrimination on the basis of the status of the individual in the production process is either partially compensated, or aggravated, so much so that it is experienced in different ways. Consequently, the horizontal lines of conflict between the 'rich' and the 'poor' become less significant politically.

Wide social disparities between the 'rich' and the 'poor' on the basis of the position they occupy in the production and distribution process render the development of national solidarity more difficult. However, the prevalence of such disparities could also promote national solidarity as and when such conflicts are exposed. Moreover, on their being recognised as 'conflicts of distribution', these conflicts are open to resolution through production increases. Horizontal solidarity within classes cuts across the divisions wrought by social segmentation, thereby facilitating nation-building. It has often been described how the 'counter-integration' of the working-class against capital and the state constituted an important element of national integration in Western Europe. The working-class organised itself on the national front, declared the national bourgeoisie to be the adversary, carried on its struggles within the national context and induced reforms at the national level. In effect, it identified itself with the national society and the Nation State, both of which it changed through its struggles. However, such a manner of effecting national integration, by breaking up the divisions of segmentation through class struggles, is difficult to pursue in the countries of the South. This is due to two reasons: First, the characteristics of historical modes of resistance against dependence on the North and second, the political structures which emerge in the wake of attempts to overcome underdevelopment.

HISTORICAL MODES OF RESISTANCE IN THE THIRD WORLD: THE FOUNDATIONS OF NATIONALISM

Constant attempts at resistance from the Third World accompanied the 'European Conquest of the World' which was undertaken in three major waves, namely, the occupation of Latin America in the sixteenth century as a byproduct of the quest for a sea-route to India; the conquest of India and Indonesia in the seventeenth and eighteenth centuries; and lastly, the colonial dismemberment of the as yet unoccupied areas of Africa and Asia, with the exception of those areas whose control was an issue of contention between the Western countries, for example, China, Iran, Afghanistan, and Thailand. These attempts at resistance are, on the whole, categorised under primary resistance and secondary resistance.

Primary resistance is understood to take the form of social movements led by traditional ruling classes, whereas secondary resistance takes the form of 'national' movements, in which participate the market-oriented middle farmers, the newly emergent class of urban workers, those employed in the informal sector, all of whom are often referred to as 'the common people', the 'new' middle classes and, for that matter, even the soldiers recruited by the colonial powers (the Sepoy Mutiny in India, 1857–58).

Primary resistance is offered by societies with collective and tributary modes of production. It has been said of communal modes of production that intensive efforts were made towards 'modernisation', as is borne out by reports from North America (the Indian Wars of the eighteenth and nineteenth centuries in the USA), South America (the Arauco Indians in Chile in the seventeenth century), and Africa. Political systems and military command networks were organised. Arms technology and even the system of education (the development of a written language in the case of the Cherokee Indians in North America), were upgraded or developed. There were innumerable cases of 'borrowing' from the Europeans, as for instance the use of the horse and the import of modern weapons. So much so, that in 1890, the occupation of Africa could be embarked upon only after the European powers had assured themselves that no more arms would be sold to African societies.

Societies with communal modes of production were also in a position to employ guerilla tactics, as is demonstrated by the collective resistance of different West African peoples organised by Samory between 1881 and 1898. The military superiority coupled with the ruthlessness of the colonists, who, until the twentieth century, had negated the applicability of their 'international law' in their dealings with such societies—in particular, to their adoption of genocide and economic warfare, broke the back of the resistance. Besides, the individual peoples who offered resistance to colonisation or expulsion were, in keeping with social development, often small in number. Rivalry between neighbouring peoples could be exploited. Individual ethnic groups, especially those which were already characterised by a relatively more advanced state of social differentiation, could profit from their connections with the Europeans. For example, the Ashanti in the Ghana of today took to hunting slaves whom they traded profitably with the Europeans. The weapons received in exchange enabled them to pursue this 'trade', for the Ashanti had, at the same time, cut off the supply of weapons to other peoples of the region.

Even those sections of the population thrown together as a result of European colonisation, namely, the cross-section of Africans exported as slaves to America, not only put up passive resistance (in the form of suicide, refusal to work), but also active resistance. The history of slavery in the modern age is, simultaneously, the history of slave uprisings. In the seventeenth century, the British preferred slaves being brought into the Antilles to be purchased from different regions of Africa, so as to make communication between them impossible. Slave uprisings and the diaspora of slaves led to the creation of slave republics in far-flung areas—this was evidenced as early as from the sixteenth century onwards in Central America, and particularly, in the eighteenth century in Brazil.

Resistance in tributary modes of production was hindered by conflicts within dominant State–classes and by the intra-societal divide between the peasants, on the one side and the State–classes, on the other. Often, as during the conquest of Mexico at the beginning of the sixteenth century, the subjugated peasant class had been newly 'absorbed' into the Empire of the respective State-classes, as a result of, and immediately preceding, the conquest. Consequently, the peasant class hailed the European invaders as liberators. Often, however, the peasants offered resistance to the attempts of the State–class to raise taxes, the rise in taxes being proposed to meet the dual objective of financing their luxury consumption and of meeting the costs of suppressing resistance.

In a few cases, the State–classes, led by their own lower ranks

(Vietnam, 1885–1900), or by leaders resolved to effect social re-organisation (Abdelkader in Algeria 1830–47), succeeded in actually mobilising the peasants for guerilla warfare. However, as soon as new avenues of self-enrichment through contact with the Europeans grew noticeably large, the State–classes lost all semblance of solidarity. Thus, all the above-mentioned forms of primary resistance refute the impression conveyed by history books that the peoples of the South were incapable of organising themselves into a state.

Partial incorporation of these tributary modes of production into the capitalist world-system (the demonstration effect, economic and social changes induced by an increase in export production, the systems of education under colonial rule) also served to enhance opportunities for organised resistance against dependence and discrimination in the Third World.

Resistance of a socio-revolutionary nature, combining traditional and European elements, can be traced to a very early date with the Taiping Revolt in China (1851–64, in which several million died). But, on the whole, the numerical strength of the new classes which emerged through contact with the West was, at first, quite small, as a result of which *secondary resistance* before 1914 was considerably weak. The widespread belief that Europe was militarily—and from the stand-point of military technology —far superior was shaken at its very foundations for the first time in 1905, with the Japanese victory over the Russian fleet.

The roots of Islamic reformism can be traced back to even before 1914—in both the case of intellectuals such as Al Afghani (1883), as also the case of political movements in Iran (which ultimately led to the Constitution of 1906), and in Indonesia (culminating in the founding of Sarekat Islam in 1912). The pre-1914 period also witnessed the growth of the Indian National Congress (established in 1885), and the birth of the first Pan--African movements (which Afro-Americans first cited as illustrative of the impact of Western elements in the Third World), the intellectual opposition in China (from 1900 onwards the government encouraged studies in Japan), which led to the Revolution of 1911, and the Mexican Revolution of 1910.

The national movements of the Third World received a powerful impetus through the First World War and the October Revolution of 1917. Europe's standing in the world received a severe jolt. President Wilson of the United States proclaimed the right of all people to self-determination, although this right was intially only confined to Europe. In Russia, the Bolsheviks, who were even more stridently anti-colonialistic, came to power.

In many countries of Asia, strong nationalist trends can be traced from 1920 onwards. In Black Africa, the resistance movement was initially not organised within the territories created by the colonial powers, but rather, the organisation was at the political level with a Pan-African objective, although its impact was quite restricted. On the other hand, tendencies to insulate oneself from white domination through the establishment of African national churches, which synthesized Christianity with African thought, were more strongly in evidence. In Asia, the rise of nationalist movements was also linked with social conflicts, as illustrated by mass peasant movements in India at the beginning of the twenties, and the revitalisation of the proletarian movement in China.

These movements, for the most part, could not make use of the communist parties, which had emerged in individual Third World countries. At the Fifth Congress of the Communist International in 1924, Lenin had decreed that communists in the areas totally or partially under colonial rule should not primarily engage themselves in organising the class struggle of the peasants and the workers against the bourgeoisie and the feudal lords, but should throw in their lot with the bourgeoisie in the struggle to attain political and economic independence within the framework of a national democratic state. Within the anti-imperialist bloc strived for, the non-communist, nationalist intelligentsia held sway. Initially, socio-revolutionary trends within Asian nationalism, which had been spawned by the October Revolution, culminated in spectacular fashion in the suppression of the proletarian uprising in Shanghai in 1927, and the retreat of the Chinese Communist Party after the so-called Long March to the rural areas of Northern China.

The wave of nationalism in the Third World which, initially, showed a tendency to ebb or stagnate in the mid-twenties, received a new fillip from the world recession of the thirties. The fall in the imports of the industrial countries resulted in a more than 50 per cent decline in commodity prices, while the terms of trade fell by a third, and the import capacity by 40 per cent. In Latin America, social movements led to the formation of populist regimes in the thirties, some, during the recession itself, and others, immediately in its wake. To be sure, these regimes also drew their support from the local ruling classes, but they pursued what was by and large a systematic policy of import-substitution. England relaxed its hold over the Arab States and India. Egypt (1922–36) and Iran (1930–32) became politically independent. The Indian nationalists secured the right to greater participation in internal affairs (1935).

However, it was only after the world economic recession, in the second half of the thirties, that the nationalist resistance movement of the Third World gathered impetus, and manifested itself in the form of mass labour strikes and marketing boycotts by peasants. The world communist movement was no longer in a position to exert a strong influence on the emerging nationalistic movement, as compared to the twenties. This was due to the fact that, since 1935, the Soviet Union had reoriented its world strategy on the basis of two objectives: It wanted to check fascism in Europe and Asia by co-operating with the Western colonial powers within the framework of the League of Nations. Moreover, it wished to fight fascism in the individual capitalist countries by joining forces with the Social Democrats and the bourgeois leftist parties ('People's Front Policy' of 1935). To support the anti-colonialist movements in the Third World would have only hampered the success of this policy.

The nationalist movements of the thirties in Third World countries were, therefore, led by primarily nationalistic leaders who were, by and large, advocates of social reform. Further, these leaders ensured the participation of all the social groups in their respective countries in the struggle for political and economic independence. Such was the political maturity of these organizations that, barring a few exceptions (Iraq in 1941, Iran in 1941, and the Indian National Congress member, Bose), these organisations did not seek to sabotage the war efforts of the Western Allies against the fascist powers and Japan. They, however, made themselves heard during the final phase of the war and demanded political independence for their countries in return for their restraint, invoking the Anglo-American Atlantic Charter (1941) and not only for tactical reasons.

In view of the vulnerability of the Western colonial powers in the post-war years, the nationalist movements in most of the

Asiatic countries were successful. The attempts of the West to use military means, not to defend the colonial system as such, but to restrict the impact of independence by transferring political power to traditional 'elites' failed in Indonesia (1945–49) and in Indo-China after a seven-year war (1947–54), but, on the other hand, were successful in Malaysia (1947–54), and in the Philippines (1946–52).

Nevertheless, outside China and Indo-China, the Western powers succeeded in stemming the socio-revolutionary trend of the time, by supporting the most modern elements amongst the nationalists. As against this, in Africa, the European colonial powers tried to at least defer the award of national independence to the territories created by them, until the end of the fifties. However, they did make continued efforts towards the economic development of those territories, development costs in relation to their national income being at that time considerably higher than the proportion of development aid today.

The concept of the non-alignment of Afro-Asian countries, initiated primarily by India, has created a certain degree of solidarity among these countries since 1955. In the fifties, the sphere of influence of these countries seemed to far exceed their actual powers. At that time, they successfully spearheaded the national awakening of all colonially ruled countries and stood out as the chief initiators of a world-wide revolution encompassing all of the South. They earned credibility in the international arena as nations whose solidarity would, in the long run, be a determining factor in the foreign policies of the countries of the South.

The USA, the leading nation of the West, saw, in the nationalist leaders, the future leaders of those countries still under colonial yoke. This was the reason why the USA insisted on a controlled mode of decolonisation, even for Africa, with the objective of stemming the socio-revolutionary tides sweeping these colonies. Interestingly, the more powerful amongst the colonial powers, in particular, had to submit to this demand, for these countries had strong interests in the South even outside of their colonies. Moreover, they also realised that by holding on to the colonial system, they would only radicalise the anti-colonial movements. Due to the weakened state of their economies after the Second World War, the colonial powers were no longer in a position to seal the colonies against the USA. While all the Western countries profited from colonial rule, the colonial powers were alone left to bear the costs of economically efficient reform policies. This had a detrimental effect on their most modern industries for which not only did the colonies fail to provide markets, but also whose international competitiveness was simultaneously eroded by the costs of colonial reform policies.

Thus, in most of the cases in Africa, political independence was granted, and power handed over to the moderate elite—who had led the nationalist anti-colonial movements—without bitter military conflicts. There are, however, glaring exceptions here, such as Algeria (1954–62), Kenya (1952–56), Zimbabwe (1965–80) as also the Portuguese colonies (1961–74). In the first three cases, European settlers attempted to stem the process of decolonisation. Stripped of her colonies, Portugal had no option but to join the ranks of the underdeveloped countries as a country of no influence. It was only in exceptional cases that the nationalists in Africa, felt compelled to adopt guerilla warfare, mobilising the mass of the rural population in the process. For the very reason that political independence was secured with relative ease in the post-1945 period, the new middle classes were almost always assigned a key role in the nationalist movements, which were based on broad class alliances.

Consequently, the lower classes hardly had a role to play in intra-societal class conflicts. Rather, this class alliance was subsumed by a nationalist ideology which suppressed intra-societal conflicts and, instead, combined traditional culture and life-style—preserving elements with Western socio-reformative and socio-revolutionary elements in varying degrees of importance. This ideology served the process of Westernisation to the extent that it sought to suppress particularisms in the interest of national unity and modernisation. Generally, such an ideology has been, and still is, anti-capitalistic in nature because it has to depict political and economic dependence as being imposed from outside and not as a situation created by factors within. Therefore, all nationalist movements in the Third World adopt etatist concepts in their economic and social policies at an early date (Arab, African or Islamic socialism), with differences in the degree to which they deem intra-societal structural change necessary, at least as professed in official promulgations.

THE FORMATION OF BUREAUCRATIC DEVELOPMENT SOCIETIES UNDER STATE–CLASSES

In all Third World societies, the state's share of the GNP, of investment in the modern sector, and of employment, is high. This is also the case in countries such as Brazil which are often regarded as being capitalist. State GNP–shares, which are low in relation to those of the capitalist industrial countries, are only to be found in poor countries in which the state can appropriate very little, due to a low level of production, and in which modern industry remains at an especially low level of development. Besides, the state also intervenes to a considerable extent in the private sector through a variety of individual measures.

It is not only the etatist orientation of the new middle class which serves as a basis for the expansion of state intervention but also the fact that investment opportunities are restricted on account of structural heterogeneity. There is a lack of mass markets, a situation which cannot be redressed by a mere redistribution of income. If the price system indicates that only a few remunerative investment avenues are open to private entrepreneurs, then available investment funds in a market-regulated economy will not be invested, or potential surplus may not be produced at all.

The expansion of the public sector in the Third World takes place on the basis of insufficient accumulation in the modern private sector. It is linked with the expansion of a class of civil servants, politicians, managers of state enterprises, and leaders of state-controlled mass organisations, (parties, trade unions and farmers' associations). Unlike the capitalists, this class does not appropriate surplus product on the strength of its competitiveness on the market, but through the instruments of state economic policy. Investment decisions are not motivated by profit expectations, rather, they are the outcome of a political process within this class. I shall refer to this class as the 'State–class' because it uses its control over the state apparatus to appropriate the mass of the surplus product and decides in which form it will be employed within the framework of political conflict. Further, in order to be a member of this class, one has to hold an office in the state apparatus or in one of the organisations closely linked with it.

The emergence of State–classes and the restructuring of societies in the South into State–class-dominated bureaucratic development societies constitutes a social factor of crucial importance for the relationship between the West and the developing countries today. The reason for this is that the vested interests of these State–classes determine both the willingness of the South to cooperate with the West, as also the nature of the concrete demands put forth by the countries of the South.

State–classes constitute both an opportunity and a danger for overcoming underdevelopment. They provide an opportunity in that they can utilise investment funds for a long-term reorientation of the productive apparatus to mass consumption. They pose a danger because they can neither be economically controlled by the market, nor politically restrained, since they have access to coercive measures and the mass of the surplus product, with the result that all other social classes are clientistically bound to them. The depoliticisation of independent trade unions, the subordination of liberation movements by transforming them into single united parties headed by the core of State–class leadership, the establishment of mass organizations for peasants, the youth, workers, women, etc., with the objective of bringing likely elements of protest under control, the dependence of private and even foreign companies on the benevolence of state bodies—all these are illustrative of 'this modern system of patronage.'

The orientation given to economic policies in bureaucratic development societies depends on the political processes within the State–class. Members of State–classes strive to increase their influence, prestige and incomes—in varying orders of precedence —with the aim of enhancing their position within their class. To achieve this, alliances with other reliable members become necessary. This creates several segments all vying with each other, which can be referred to as cliques or clans. This rivalry, in turn, gives rise to a tendency to squander resources.

Each segment can enhance the power, prestige and incomes of its members by participating in the expansion of consumer expenditures, in cooperation with other segments, rather than by attempting to curtail the resources of other segments in its own favour. This self-serving nature of these aims gradually proves to be a drain on the capacity for spending. At the same time, State–classes in the Third World of today are subject to a new compulsion to legitimise. Unlike State–classes in tributary modes of production, these State–classes cannot claim religious legitimacy. Their ascent to power is usually marked by the claim of overcoming underdevelopment and are, therefore, committed, at least verbally, to development goals. They should, at least, give the impression of pursuing these goals.

This compulsion to serve one's own interest and the need to acquire legitimacy lead to a cyclic development of the policies of State–classes in bureaucratic development societies. Dominant segments are in a position to ensure greater privileges for themselves, and they make this policy secure by allying themselves with other social groups. Allies are all the more invaluable if they have resources of their own (foreign companies, local groups with resources, local entrepreneurs, agricultural capitalists). Since the available number of such partners is quite restricted, rival segments have, at times, to rest content with the support of none else but the underprivileged. To ensure their own rise to power, these segments evolve programmes, on behalf of, and in the interest of, the poor. If they are successful in dislodging hitherto dominant segments, by playing on, for example, the latter's economic problems, the tendency towards self-serving is, at least temporarily, curtailed. Opportunities for reform are created, as a matter of fact, through the efforts of the dominant segments to ward off such attempts at reform : State–classes can forsee a crisis and are 'capable of reform'. There emerges a cyclic movement, with 'an (established) segment of the ruling class being regularly over-thrown by a more idealistic, younger segment' (Sklar, 1967:8), with the middle ranks of the army, the civil administration, the mass organisations, and the state party playing an important role in the process.

The extent to which mass interests are actually considered in this cyclic movement, and not merely paid lip service to, does not depend very much on the origins or ideology of State–class segments, for, at the very latest by the second generation of this class (which reproduces itself in the secondary school system), the 'revolutionary' capital available from liberation movements faces the threat of extinction. Segments which are determined to overcome underdevelopment through mass production for mass consumption using their own technology, are more likely to be supported or tolerated by other segments if it appears possible to reorient the productive apparatus to meet a growing mass demand. Whoever produces bicycles, transistor radios, or fertilisers is allowed to concentrate on the increasing mass demand.

The often incidental promotion of projects, which can be accommodated within a strategy geared to mass consumption needs, facilitates the implementation of a strategy for restructuring the productive apparatus, although this objective was not pursued at the outset. The development policy of the West, therefore, has a bearing on the political processes within State–classes.

The restructuring of the societies of the South into bureaucratic development societies has had important implications for West–South relations. The State–classes of the South, now in a position to regulate the State's policy of external relations, frequently put forth demands to the West. In fact, within the State–classes itself, rival segments find no difficulty in arriving at a consensus on the issue of financial demands to be made of the industrial West. The argument attributing underdevelopment to the state of dependency on the West, a state created by the West, serves the interests of both the more socio-revolutionary segments as well as the more pro-West ones, for this argument is used as a justification for the absence of structural reforms in the interest of the poor in the Third World. By employing moral arguments and threatening to join forces with the East, these segments can hope to enhance their capacity to extract concessions from the West. Further, verbal 'anti-imperialism' and successes on the foreign economic front allow internal protest to be vented on foreign 'scape-goats'.

As an outcome of the position occupied by State–classes within the societies of the South, the problem of overcoming under-development is being increasingly viewed as a problem concerning international economic relations. In order to force the West to focus its attention on this simplified definition of the problem, the State–classes of the South adopt strategies towards the West which combine the elements of cooperation and conflict. For, only through cooperation can the maximum amount of concessions be extracted from the partner.

3

The Politico-Economic Foundations of North–South Relations

The economic demands of the countries of the South, or rather of their ruling State–classes, constitute a topic of deliberation in the North–South dialogue. These demands stem from the overlapping objective of enhancing import opportunities. They are concretely moulded by the burdens of external trade, which themselves have resulted from the development strategies adopted so far.

THE PROBLEM OF COMMODITY EXPORTS FROM THE SOUTH

The Third World's share of world raw material supplies is grossly overestimated.

The industrial countries are net exporters of foodstuffs. Of the 1787 billion tonnes of foodgrain produced all over the world in 1987, the developed capitalist countries—with 14.5 per cent of the world population and an agricultural labour force of 24 million—accounted for 31.6 per cent whereas only 29.5 per cent was produced in the developing 'market economies' (all Third World countries with the exception of China, Mongolia, North Korea, Vietnam, Laos and Cambodia), which account for almost 52 per cent of the world population and with an agricultural work-force of 432 million. Per capita food production in the less

TABLE 3

World Trade in Food Grains (Millions of $)

	1965	1970	1975	1979	1981	1985	1987
Exports of developing market economies	1473	1110	781	3695	5807	4834	3205
Imports of developing market economies	1946	2314	8709	10393	15435	10214	9672
OPEC	188	314	1771	3022	4335	3144	3052

developed countries (excluding China and India) rose by 11 per cent from 1969/71 to 1979/81 and rose only by 2 per cent until 1986, with middle-income countries registering a 10 per cent increase. Thus, the Third World continues to be dependent on the food production of the industrialised countries (Table 3).

In the case of mineral raw materials, the Third World's share of world production is noteworthy only in the case of a few select minerals: zinc, manganese, nickel and crude oil. However, the facts do go to show (see Table 4) that the Third World's share has undergone an enormous increase when compared to its share at the beginning of the century, when the West, for the most part, accounted for over 90 per cent of mineral raw material production (lower shares only in the case of copper and zinc).

Even in energy production, the Third World plays a role of limited importance. High shares were once observable for crude oil production but are now declining: OPEC 1987, 31 per cent; 1980, 45 per cent; 1973, 52 per cent; Third World 1987, 46 per cent; 1980, 55 per cent; 1973, 59 per cent; (the share of non-OPEC Third World countries rose from 6.7 per cent to 9.4 per cent in 1980 and to 14.1 per cent in 1987). By contrast, the OPEC's share of world energy production in 1980—in the face of the North's domination in the production of coal and natural gas—amounted to just about 22.6 per cent, declining in 1985 to 13.2 per cent. OPEC's share of energy production outside the communist countries amounted to 38.2 per cent in 1980 and 20.9 per cent in 1985 as compared to the 1973 figures of 28.8 per cent and 42.6 per cent, respectively.

TABLE 4

Percentage Share of Third World in World Mineral Production

	1961	1970	1980	1986
Coal	13.3	19.4	33.1	34.3
Lignite	1.0	1.9	3.3	8.2
Crude oil	48.1	58.9	58.7	47.3
Iron*	21.5	19.4	38.2	28.3
Bauxite	69.7	58.4	48.1	61.3
Lead*	34.5	26.1	30.9	21.1
Zinc*	31.8	26.2	27.6	28.3
Tin*	86.0	83.3	84.4	66.3
Manganese*	56.0	60.9	58.7	28.5
Chromium*	32.9	37.1	60.5	19.0 [2]
Nickel*	19.3	32.8	37.2	19.1
Natural Phosphate	38.9	37.0	40.6	38.0
Uranium*	n.a.	25.4 [1]	35.1	22.8 [3]
Copper	42.5	40.0	44.6	45.5

Source : UN, Commodity Production Data.

N.B.: Third World = Asia, Africa, Latin America, excluding Japan and Asiatic USSR.

   * Metal Content in each case.

1 1971.

2 1984.

3 1985.

In the case of raw materials for which the Third World's share of world production is high, (percentages denote share of production in the South, 1980), the lion's share of production is accounted for by just two countries in each case (bauxite: Jamaica and Guinea 55.8 per cent; tin: Malaysia and Thailand 53.3 per cent; manganese: South Africa and Gabon: 61.6 per cent; chromium: South Africa 58.5 per cent; Zimbabwe 10.4 per cent). Here, it is mostly countries which are regarded to be politically stable which account for these major shares. This is once again reemphasized by the list of the most important—in terms of export value, excluding oil—primary exporters of the Third World at the end of the 1970s (Chile, Brazil, Zambia, Peru, Malaysia, Zaire, Morocco, Philippines, Thailand, Indonesia). In 1986 this list reads as follows: Brazil, Cuba, Malaysia, Argentina, Thailand, Indonesia, Mexico, Columbia, India.

This fact of the limited importance of the South as a producer of mineral raw materials and, in particular, the concentration of commodity production in the hands of a few countries is not contradicted by the developing countries' high share of commodity exports (1978–80, and 1984 figures in percentage): crude oil: 86.6 and 74.0; bauxite: 84.3 and 83.4; tin: 81.1 and 69.2; manganese: 77.8 and 50.2; phosphate: 65.3 and 60.5; copper: 61.5 and 65.5; iron: 43.1 and 39.7).

In the case of agricultural commodities from the Third World, the South's share of tropical products in world exports is naturally high due to the climatic advantages it enjoys. However, only a few of these commodities make up a significant proportion of world trade. Important items of agricultural commodity export from the Third World include tropical beverages (coffee, cocoa and tea, to the tune of $ 15.3 billion in 1979, making up almost one-fourth, and $ 14.3 billion in 1983–84) apart from oilseeds and nuts and the by-products of their first processing (a good sixth in 1979, 1983–84 $ 4.9 billion in 1983–84, making up one-eighth); whilst fibres, even taking into account their first processing into jute and cotton fabric, accounted for just about one-tenth in 1979, but declined by 1985 to one-twelfth through declining quantities and falling prices. Fruits made up less than one-fifteenth of the export value of agricultural products in 1979, and one-tenth in 1983–84. The export of oilseeds and nuts, sugar (having a higher export value than all fibres), fibres and wood is subject to severe competition from non-Third World producers or is constrained by protectionist measures resorted to by the industrial countries. Although the Third World's share of commodity exports (excluding oil) is declining, this still continues to be its major source of foreign exchange.

In 1979, the Third World exported goods to the tune of $ 418 billion, of which fuel made up $ 236 billion and manufactures $ 83 billion. Commodity exports were to the tune of $ 100 billion, out of which mineral raw materials including smelted ores amounted to $ 35 billion, agricultural commodities and foodstuffs to the extent identifiable, $ 65 billion. The most important mineral raw materials are copper and copper concentrates (accounting for 3.1 per cent of the exports, excluding crude oil), iron ore (1.5 per cent), tin (1.3 per cent) and bauxite with the byproducts of its first processing (0.8 per cent).

Exports in 1985 amounted to $ 463 billion, of which fuel made up $ 195 billion and manufactures $ 150 billion. Commodity exports were still to the tune of $ 99 billion, of which ores and scraps had dramatically fallen to $ 25 billion, whereas agricultural commodities and foodstuffs amounted to $ 78 billion. Copper and copper concentrates remained the major mineral export materials (now accounting for 1.1 per cent of total exports, excluding crude oil and petroleum products), followed closely by iron ore (1.1 per cent), and bauxite with the byproducts of its first processing (0.9 per cent).

It is the less developed countries which are most dependent on the export of agricultural commodities: In 1979, they still drew as much as 53 per cent of their export earnings from agricultural commodities (excluding China and India), and as much as 65 per cent after deducting the value of fuels and metals from the total export value (1960: 90 per cent). The share of agricultural commodities in exports has declined due to increasing export of products from countries as Pakistan or Bangladesh, though only to 47 per cent. However, calculated in terms of the criteria of non-minerals and non-fuel exports, this share remains as high as 59 per cent. By comparison, the middle-income countries draw only about 20 per cent of their export earnings from this sector and if minerals and fuels are excluded, 28 per cent.

It is the smaller and less developed countries which continue to be dependent on the export of agricultural commodities to a substantial degree: by over 80 per cent. These countries include, above all, African countries, such as Chad (share of agricultural commodities as a percentage of total merchandise export (in 1976: 96), Somalia (99), Mali (99), Burundi (99), Ruanda (99), Burkina Fasso (87), Malawi (96), Mozambique (86), Uganda (96), Sudan (96), Ghana (86), Madagascar (82), and Central American countries such as the Honduras (85), Nicaragua (87) and Cuba (94), as also Burma (93). As many as forty countries of the Third World are·dependent on the export of agricultural products by over 50 per cent, although this number has been increased by the independence of small island states. Poor marketing conditions for agricultural products have reduced their share in exports, whereas in a number of larger countries diversification increased since the 1980s. For several countries, individual tropical agricultural products make a vital contribution to export earnings. This is particularly true in the case of coffee, which brings in over 25 per cent of the export earnings of eleven Third World countries (1984).

In view of the high prices fetched by crude oil until 1985, oil-exporting countries are heavily dependent on this raw material for their foreign exchange earnings. This is so even in the case of densely populated countries with diversified economic structures (Mexico, 1978–80: 61 per cent. 1984, 68 per cent; Indonesia, 1978–80: 63 per cent, 1985, 49 per cent; Egypt, 1978–80, 58 per cent, 1986, 51 per cent).

Even in the case of other mineral exports, there is a concentration of foreign exchange earnings from one single product, as for example, from uranium in Niger (87 per cent, 1982); iron in Mauretania (49 per cent, 1984) and Liberia (62 per cent, 1982); tin in Bolivia (60 per cent in the 1970s, now replaced by natural gas); from copper and other non-ferrous metals derived in the course of copper production in Chile (49 per cent in the 1970s, 38 per cent in 1986, due to fruit and other agricultural exports), Zaire (35 per cent, 1978), Zambia (93 per cent, 1982) and Peru (in the 1970s, now diversified through other exports of non-ferrous metals), despite crude oil exports in this case; from bauxite and byproducts of its first processing in Surinam (57 per cent), Jamaica (65 per cent, 1984), Guyana (45 per cent, 1979).

Dependence on commodity exports has far-reaching consequences for development planning. Unlike in the case of manufactured goods, developing countries have, for a long time, been competitive in the market for raw materials. Commodity exports have been taxed by Third World governments, not only since 1973 but as far back as from the end of the nineteenth century (Guano in Peru), and subsequently, to a greater extent, since the world economic recession of the thirties. Critics of such forms of intervention that are adverse to the market would do well to recall that in the seventeenth and eighteenth centuries, Great Britain imposed heavy duties on its coal exports so as to enrich itself at the expense of its competitors.

In the case of many tropical agricultural products, agricultural producers in some Third World countries receive less than 50 per cent of the world market price. The difference flows into the state exchequer through the so-called state marketing boards, or price support funds. In Ghana, for example, the duty on cocoa yielded 49.3 per cent of state revenue in 1979; in Cameroon 63.3 per cent of the state revenue was earned from export tariffs (1979). Since the sixties, these proportions have been regressive, but this does not warrant the inference that commodity exports have grown less important for Third World state finances, but only that the mode of taxation has been changed. Considerable differences between farmgate prices and border prices continue to exist.

As soon as a state marketing board has been set up, export duties are entered as the income of a state enterprise. In the case of mineral raw materials, as with copper production in Chile in the beginning of the sixties, the level of export duties was over 60 per cent of the world price. However, as soon as production is taken over by state enterprises, this revenue goes into the state exchequer not as revenue from taxes but as profit, and is, therefore, difficult to quantify. What is of crucial significance, though, is the fact that for many of the medium and smaller countries, duties on commodity exports, or on exports, in general, constitute the most important source of revenue. This explains why all Third World governments are interested in good commodity prices.

Most commodity exports generate little employment. In the case of coffee, the most important tropical agricultural product in terms of value, the number of peasant families and rural labourers employed during the sixtees was estimated at four million. In mining, employment generation is lower still. In this sector, the number of people employed in the eleven most important mining countries of the Third World (in terms of their export value), amounted to just about 1.4 million in the second half of the eighties, this including all workers in such important and labour-intensive activities such as quarrying.

Employment may be generated by the processing of agricultural commodities. In the case of mineral products, processing would create just a little under one million jobs at an investment level of $ 180 billion. Thus, almost $ 180,000 has to be invested to create one job, i.e., four times as much as in the industrial sector of the Federal Republic of Germany. The processing of natural gas and crude oil in the Arab oil-producing countries is competitive only when the supply of the raw materials is at prime cost, and not at the world market price. The technical learning effects are but few in the case of raw material processing, since local labour does not acquire complete mastery over the generally imported capital-intensive technology.

The argument that *developing countries feel disadvantaged in the area of commodity export because the purchasing power of their commodity exports has fallen in relation to the cost of their imports, is, from the statistical point of view, a disputable one*. Depending

on the base year, and in view of the—albeit overestimated—fluctuations in commodity prices, a worsening in the terms of the trade
between Third World commodity exports and Third World industrial goods imports could either be substantiated or refuted.
However, the thesis of steady terms of trade misses the essence of
the argument advanced by H.W. Singer, who points not to the
discrimination of the primary producing countries, but of the
underdeveloped countries, which results from the social conditions
of the process of price formation in the industrial and developing
countries. An equal exchange takes place if, after taking into
account the difference in levels of capital investment, the prices of
goods and services develop in such a manner that wage incomes in
the various branches of production are equal within certain bands.
Goods and services from production branches, whose rise in productivity is slower than the average rate of the economy, will,
relatively, be more expensive, as compared to other goods.

A prerequisite for such a process of adjustment is the mobility of
labour between the various branches of production. However, the
migration of cheap labour from the Third World into the industrial
countries is prohibited, with the result that a homogeneous international labour market does not exist. The price formation for raw
materials from the Third World, and industrial goods from the
West, rests on conditions of immobility of labour. In the West,
employees make use of social processes (collective bargaining),
and economic processes (the trend towards full employment)
to participate in productivity increases, in terms of rising real
incomes. Compared to this, widespread unemployment in the
South is the cause for rising productivity in export production
leading, in turn, to price decreases. These price decreases can
only be conditionally offset by an increase in output quantity.
An important aspect of productivity increase in a capitalistic
system is economy of material and not, by any means, the wastage
of raw material. Besides, at rising levels of consumer income,
there is a smaller increase in demand for foodstuffs. It is for this
reason that the demand for raw materials and foodstuffs in the
industrialised countries of the West rises more slowly than the GNP.

In the case of mineral raw materials only alumina (a byproduct
of bauxite processing), nickel and iron ore register sizeable increases in quantities exported between 1961 and 1979. In the
case of tropical beverages, which constitute important earners

TABLE 5

Changes in Quantity and Nominal and Real Incomes for Some Important Third World Commodity Exports
(export value over $1 billion in 1979, or nominal increase in export of over 200 per cent)

	Revenue in 1979 (in million $)	Increase in Quantity (%)	Increase in Nominal Revenue (%)	Increase in Real Revenue (%)	Increase in Revenue Per Real Unit of Quantity*
Cocoa	2802	– 11.0	+ 484	+ 175	+ 196
Tin	2438	+ 14.3	+ 630	+ 222	+ 181
Coffee	11262	+ 36.2	+ 525	+ 176	+ 102
Beef	1361	+ 49.6	+ 583	+ 201	+ 101
Fish (frozen or tinned)	1593	+ 346.0	+ 2010	+ 830	+ 108
Crustaceans	2287	+ 455.0	+ 2377	+ 992	+ 97
Bauxite	612	+ 65.4	+ 581	+ 200	+ 81
Palm kernel oil	260	+ 446.8	+ 2029	+ 838	+ 69
Coconut oil	952	+ 277.7	+ 1438	+ 534	+ 68
Nickel	563	+ 208.7	+ 902	+ 381	+ 66
Oranges	1499	+ 88.0	+ 556	+ 189	+ 54
Wood	5116	+ 211.5	+ 880	+ 332	+ 39
Oil cakes	2106	+ 249.4	+ 988	+ 379	+ 37
Copper	5600	+ 79.7	+ 455	+ 145	+ 36
Rock phosphate	1080	+ 146.6	+ 640	+ 226	+ 32
Soyabeans	992	+ 3494.6	+ 9923	+ 4319	+ 26
Alumina	907	+ 274.0	+ 936	+ 356	+ 22
Rice	1867	+ 29.6	+ 256	+ 57	+ 21
Palm oil	1138	+ 213.5	+ 823	+ 307	+ 30
Sugar	2912	+ 41.2	+ 234	+ 47	+ 10
Cotton	3127	+ 4.5	+ 150	+ 11	+ 6

TABLE 5 (Contd.)

	Revenue in 1979 (in million $)	Increase in Quantity (%)	Increase in Nominal Revenue (%)	Increase in Real Revenue (%)	Increase in Revenue Per Real Unit of Quantity*
Maize	1269	+ 144.0	+ 481	+ 156	+ 5
Soyabean oil	602	+ 6497.9	+ 15736	+ 6883	+ 5
Pepper	218	+ 111.0	+ 461	+ 103	+ 4
Tobacco	1732	+ 64.7	+ 231	+ 46	− 11
Bananas	1052	+ 74.5	+ 227	+ 44	− 18
Iron ore	2697	+ 172.3	+ 407	+ 123	− 18
Sorghum	438	+ 552.1	+ 1025	+ 352	− 31
Manganese	380	+ 98.0	+ 244	+ 53	− 24
Rubber	3968	+ 60.0	+ 247	+ 9	− 32
Tea	833	+ 35.9	+ 109	− 8	− 32

Source : Computed on the basis of UN Commodity Trade and Price Trends 1980.
* Based on the US Price Index for Machinery and Equipment (1980).

of foreign exchange, increases in quantity are but small; for cocoa, the trend is even regressive. In the case of oilseeds and nuts, the quantities recorded reveal an increase of 225 per cent, while the oil-content of these exports rose by 400 per cent in view of the higher degree of processing. However, in nominal terms, revenue rose only by 456 per cent. With the prices of capital goods increasing by 226 per cent in the period 1961–79, the purchasing power of animal and vegetable oil exports doubled, although the purchasing power per unit of quantity actually decreased by 50 per cent, despite a higher degree of processing.

UNCTAD data for the 1980s does not show increases in earnings from raw material exports, with minor exceptions as in the case of bananas (+ 18 per cent), tea (+ 14 per cent) and vegetable oils (+ 23 per cent). In ten of the eighteen reported commodities (bananas, bovine meat, hard fibres, jute and its manufactures, timber, bauxite, manganese, phosphate rock, and tin), quantities exported decreased. Quantities of cotton exported were stable. Quantities exported increased in the case of cocoa, coffee, sugar, tea, vegetable oil, natural rubber, copper, and iron ore. In contrast to the 1970s, in the 1980s, there were no new potentialities of raw material production in the Third World. Agricultural raw materials and minerals were more depressed than food exports.

It has rightly been observed that raw materials from the Third World are cheap because the labour invested in their production receives low wages. This, in effect, points to the problem of structural heterogeneity as an expression of underdevelopment. It is only when the Third World lags greatly behind the industrial countries in terms of technology, outside the sphere of commodity production, that it is possible for labour incomes in the Third World to stagnate despite productivity increases in the export branches, even while labour incomes in the industrial countries rise as a result of productivity increases. Otherwise, stagnating incomes in the Third World and rising incomes in the industrial countries would lead to Third World competitiveness in the case of other products.

The argument advanced by Singer and Prebisch can also be reversed. If the demand for raw material from the Third World hardly responds to a change in prices, then Third World suppliers can restrict supply by forming a cartel, so that prices are forced to rise. Such a strategy rests on two mechanisms: differential and consumer rents.

Differential rent is the income accruing to a producer who has access to more favourable natural conditions of production than his rival competitor, whose supply is just about adequate to satisfy the consumption demand. The oil-producing countries were in a position to raise the price of crude oil so as to correspond with that of alternative forms of energy, i.e., to the level of costs for producing *additional* energy in the industrial countries.

It is obvious that only the cost differentials, and not the producers' share of world production, are of consequence for such a strategy. Cost differences are to be found in the production of metals as well. Mineral ores in the Third World often contains many times the metal content of ore mined in the industrial countries, not to speak of the ore that would have to be extracted if Third World countries were to restrict their supply. Although the costs of ore extraction are comparable all the world over, a developing country needs to extract just one-third to one-seventh of the quantity of ore mined in an industrial country in order to obtain the same quantity of metal.

Consumer rent involves the operation of the following mechanism: With the increasing availability of one particular type of article, the utility value of additional quantities of the same article decreases. Many people would be ready to pay a very high price for the first cup of coffee in the day, but certainly not for the tenth. Thus, at a very low level of supply, the price at which supply and demand are balanced out is extremely high, and depending on the price elasticity of demand—i.e., the empirically observable consumer behaviour—the price falls, at first, gradually with an increase in supply, and then so rapidly that the increase in quantity sold does not offset the fall in price and in earnings. In 1976, when the supply of coffee grew scarce as a result of the outbreak of frost in Brazil, the world market price for raw coffee rose fourfold. At least in the case of West Germany, the coffee-roasters and marketing companies could shift the burden of this price rise completely onto the consumer. Despite an increase in the retail price of coffee by as much as a third, there was no decline in the coffee consumption of German households.

The above possibilities of appropriating differential and consumer rents through the monopolistic commodity price strategies adopted by the Third World countries are to be differentiated from the strategies for commodity price, or income, stabilisation currently under discussion. Commodity prices should be stabilised through the establishment of buffer stockpiles. These buffer stocks sell provisions at a fixed maximum price, thereby deflating the price; they buy up goods from the market at a fixed minimum price with the proceeds of the phase of high prices and stock them. Stabilising commodity prices through market intervention should have the effect of reducing price fluctuations, which are often the cause of complaint. Price stabilisation is undoubtedly an important objective because, often, the implementation of development projects depends on commodity income and underdeveloped, raw material-producing countries are not in a position to substitute hitherto imported goods with local products, due to the structural heterogeneity at declining commodity prices.

IMPORT-SUBSTITUTION AND THE FOREIGN EXCHANGE GAP

Import-substitution, or import-substituting industrialisation, is understood to be the commencement of production, in the developing countries, of those goods which had previously been imported. This strategy appears plausible almost immediately, since one can proceed from the assumption that there is a domestic market available for the goods hitherto imported. To a certain extent, import-substitution developed without state intervention. Expansion in commodity exports created purchasing power within the country. As a result of this, markets emerged in the larger countries, making the indigenous production of previously imported goods appear remunerative. The change-over to the local production of industrial goods always accelerated when, either difficulties in commodity export, or delivery problems from the supply side (i.e., from the industrial countries) rendered the import of industrial goods difficult.

Import-substitution is marked by certain characteristic phases: the building up of capacities for the production of simple consumer goods is followed by the change-over to durable consumer goods, and some preliminary and intermediate products. Even production plants for simple consumer goods are set up with relatively modern, imported and, therefore, capital-intensive technology.

However, since the number of jobs created here is too small to narrow down wide income disparities in the Third World, the mass demand for simple consumer goods is exhausted relatively quickly.

In the case of local products substituting imports to meet the demand of the high income groups, the narrowness of the market leads to a production series in which unit costs are often higher than prices in the world market. Trade barriers are erected in order to protect units from outside competition. Intermediate inputs, especially capital goods, are exempted from duty, so as to prevent production costs from rising too sharply. Capital is subsidised against the factor of production of labour, with the result that relatively capital-intensive methods of production are employed. This, in turn, restricts the demand for unskilled labour, with skilled labour, on the other hand, becoming scarce. The mass of unskilled labour is faced with growing unemployment, while a small number of skilled workers draw relatively high incomes.

Owing to the fact that unequal income distribution prevailed in most Third World countries right from the start, income-substituting industrialisation only gives rise to wider disparities within the working class, often compounded by a deepening of the urban–rural divide, highly inefficient unit sizes and, lastly, by the fact that the rest of the economy especially the rural population has to bear the costs of production, which are extremely high.

Capital 'deepening' combined with the low profits of inefficient enterprises, gives rise to a situation where this import-substituting sector does not, by itself, mobilise the investment funds which are necessary for further growth (the savings gap). Concentration on the production of non-durable and durable consumer goods, as also of basic inputs (steel, chemicals), in whose case cost differences vis-a-vis the industrial countries appear to be lower than for the local production of capital goods, only creates technical dependence. Indigenous capacities for technology production emerge only in exceptional cases.

Even intermediate inputs have to be adapted to the imported technology, while locally available inputs are often found to not satisfy quality requirements. Despite previously imported products being substituted by local ones, there emerges a burgeoning import demand for intermediate inputs and capital goods in the course of further industrialisation (the foreign exchange gap). Such a process of industrialisation is self-impeding, for it must either be financed by rising incomes from commodity export, or by aid from the West.

PUBLIC ENTERPRISE IN THE THIRD WORLD: INTENSIFYING AND REORIENTING IMPORT-SUBSTITUTING INDUSTRIALISATION

Since the restricted nature of the markets in the Third World renders the production of capital goods, and often even basic goods, unremunerative for private enterprises, the state often assumes the task of developing these 'bottleneck sectors'. Objectives and strategies may vary in nature. The State–class, while orienting itself to the foreign exchange deficit, could create and develop public sector capacities for the production of intermediate inputs and some capital goods for existing import–substituting industries. Public enterprises are then set up in those sectors in which a market is expected to emerge under conditions of continuing demand trends observable in the private sector, but in which local entrepreneurs are unwilling to invest, however high the level of tariff protection may be.

Alternatively, the State–class can also orient itself on the basis of an overall economic and social model, which overcomes the problems faced during import-substitution by restructuring the productive apparatus to meet mass demand. Here, we can observe two variants of the bureaucratic development society, namely, the *inegalitarian modernisation state*, so called because it follows the inegalitarian path laid out by the situation of departure; and, secondly, the *egalitarian modernising state*, so termed because it aims at the creation of mass markets through agrarian reforms, among other measures—these mass markets being characterised by a relatively homogenous demand for a few products, the restriction of investment to a few production lines and by efficient unit sizes. Reasonable as this strategy may appear to be on the macroeconomic front, microeconomically, it is difficult to implement in view of the constraints which state enterprises in both types of bureaucratic development societies are confronted with. Demand trends form the basis for the establishment of public enterprises in the first variant; in the second variant, one basis for this enterprise lies in the pattern of inter-industry relations resulting from the parallel development of state units in the country concerned.

Often, difficulties posed by planning are underestimated. This is further aggravated by the fundamental orientation to investment goals rather than to profit and production goals. The orientation to production goals is effected through empirical values, derived from other comparable units, which have demonstrated that, for instance, a certain roller mill enables a certain production output, and that this roller mill carries a certain value. These empirical values drawn from developed countries, are, for the most part, unrealistic for conditions prevailing in underdeveloped countries. As soon as difficulties in project implementation surface, the management will compare delays and failures in production goal attainment to the successes of other plants. Since problems crop up everywhere, each management will consider planning targets in perceived intra-industrial relations as unrealistic. This reinforces the tendency to resolve difficulties in conjunction with foreign partners.

Another way of averting the dreaded threat of input scarcity is to build up one's own production capacities outside the framework of the original plan in the projected unit. The outcome is a self-integration of the public enterprise concerned, effected at high capital costs, and an unplanned-for increase in the utilisation of foreign technologies, instead of the national interlinkage of the industrial sector, as originally planned.

The moment public enterprises are set up because investment is unremunerative, profits cannot be demanded in the short term. The temptation to resolve efficiency-related problems by dipping into the state exchequer is great. The argument that serves as a justification for this point, maintains that the plant performs certain tasks in the interest of the general public, for example, it brings about a change in the infrastructure and organises the training of the workers, in return for which it does not gain any income. In the light of the characteristic features of underdevelopment, these arguments are neither totally false nor wholly valid, for apart from the costs incurred by such economically necessary tasks, one must also consider the costs of 'unproductive' measures, like for instance, the engagement of workers who are not necessary for production but who, upon being engaged, bring down the level of unemployment.

A mere decentralisation of state enterprises and their subjection to market controls, leads either to their bankruptcy, to the requisite tasks being transferred onto the state (sparking off conflicts over the regional and sectoral allocation of funds for training and infrastructure), or to the decentralised public enterprises that draw heavily from public funds, thus exacerbating the tendency towards indebtedness.

Nevertheless, a certain measure of import-substitution and state economic promotion is accepted even by the proponents of greater liberalisation vis-a-vis the world market, on the grounds that it facilitates improvements in infrastructure and the training of the workers. A moderate policy of import-substitution combined with a cautious expansion of the role of the state in production could create the conditions necessary for export-oriented industrialisation.

MARKETS FOR THIRD WORLD MANUFACTURES

Since the beginning of the seventies, the contradictions inherent in import-substituting industrialisation have provoked a widespread demand for the orientation of the process of industrialisation on the basis of comparative cost advantages, or, in other words, the specialisation in labour-intensive industrial products. Specialisation on the basis of comparative cost advantages entails that a country specialises in goods for which its productivity may possibly be lower than that of its competitors, though the difference in this case is smaller than in the case of other products. It was the increase in the volume of manufactured exports from a sizeable number of Third World countries that provided the background for the theoretical discussion on export–oriented industrialisation.

If the industrial countries of the West develop in a manner in which growth in real wages is tendentially parallel to growth in productivity, unit costs rise in those branches of production with a below-average increase in labour productivity will experience a rise in unit costs. Such processes were known to have begun as early as in the nineteenth century in the manufacturing sector (India's textile industry). Following upheavals in the global economy, in the period spanning the two World Wars, rising real wages in the industrial countries, and the increasing transferability of mature technologies by then even to Third World countries, once again reactivated this process of relocating production units in the South.

Since the seventies, this process has been growing in importance: Between 1962 and 1970, Third World manufactured exports (including byproducts of the first processing of ore) rose by 16.5 per cent, p.a., between 1970 and 1978 by 28.8 per cent, p.a. (excluding smelted ores and steel and iron). By contrast, world exports of products registered a considerably slower rate of growth at 12.3 per cent, p.a. between 1962 and 1970, and at 17.5 per cent, p.a. in 1970–1978. The Third World's share of manufactured exports increased from 5.1 per cent in 1970, to 10.7 per cent in 1978, 11.0 per cent in 1982 and 14.7 per cent in 1987. Initially, textiles accounted for a major portion of these exports (34.8 per cent in 1970, 26.9 per cent in 1981). This was particularly evident in the case of the burgeoning exports from Asia—the share of textiles made up 42.5 per cent in 1970, 33.8 per cent in 1978, 30.7 per cent in 1981, 24.3 per cent in 1982 and 24.3 per cent in 1987.

TABLE 6

Export of Manufactures (Millions of $) *

	World-wide	Developing 'market economies'	%	Latin American developing countries	African Developing 'market economies'	Asian Developing 'market economies' excluding the Middle East
1962**	79,758	4,210	5.2	859	402	2,105
1970	172,868	8,849	5.1	1,648	836	6,011
1975	535,267	29,797	5.6	951	907	7,707
1978	626,900	66,829	10.7	10,560	2,340	45,576
1980	1,134,939	109,236	9.6	20,523	7,244	75,205
1982	1,072,393	118,358	11.0	19,311	5,315	83,980
1984	1,168,045	155,335	13.3	26,792	5,477	112,543
1986	1,467,997	192,247	13.0	27,795	6,702	138,053
1987	1,759,261	258,454	14.7	34,158	3,873	189,509

* Categories 5-8 SITC, excl. 6.7 = iron and steel, and 6.8 = smelted ores
** Including the by-products of the first processing of ores (Commodity category SITC 6.7 and 6.8)

Source : United Nations, Monthly Bulletin of Statistics, various issues, author's calculations.

Growth has also been recorded particularly in the exports of machinery and transport equipment (automobiles and ships), whose share of manufactured exports from Asia rose from 14.3 per cent in 1970 to 27.1 per cent in 1981, with an average annual increase of 25.3 per cent during this period, this growth in exports setting in particularly from 1975 onwards (51.2 per cent, p.a.). But in the 1980s, growth rates slowed down to 18 per cent p.a. due to the virtual stagnation between 1984 and 1986 (+7 per cent). The share of this class of products thus remained stagnant (1984, 34.7 per cent, 1987, 34.5 per cent).

These exports were concentrated among a few countries, predominantly countries of South-East and East Asia. In 1978, Hong Kong, Singapore and South Korea, by themselves, accounted for as much as 40.5 per cent (1984, 39.1 percent) of the total manufactured exports from the Third World and 56.3 per cent of the total exports of manufactures from Asia (1984, 47.5 per cent). In 1984, a considerable portion of the remaining exports of manufactured goods came from Taiwan, 19.8 per cent of Third World total, and 24.1 per cent of Asian manufacturing exports.

Despite an undeniable diversification in manufactured exports, the close of the seventies saw individual countries becoming heavily dependent on a few products: Textiles made up 44.5 per cent of Hong Kong's exports in 1977 (1983/84, 40.1 per cent), 82.8 per cent (1983/84, 72.6 per cent) of Macao's and 45.3 per cent (1983/84, 41.7 per cent) of exports from Malta. Only the exports of South Korea, Singapore, Brazil and Mexico are more widely distributed over different groups of products—in the case of South Korea, ships, shoes and electrical machines demonstrate this diverse distribution; in the case of Singapore it is electrical appliances (household gadgets, radios, TVs, cassette recorders); whereas manufactured exports from the two Latin American countries include various types of equipment, automobiles, among others.

With respect to the export of any one manufactured product, in 1977, an extremely small number of Third World countries accounted, for over 50 per cent of the total exports from this group of countries, in each case. (Figures for 1983/84 are given in brackets). Veneers, chopped wood: 69.3 per cent from South Korea, Malaysia, Singapore (59 per cent from these countries and Indonesia); leather: 71.5 per cent (57.0 per cent) from India, Argentina,

Brazil; automobiles: 56.0 per cent (48.0 per cent) from Brazil, Argentina, Kuwait; non-electrical machines: 55.2 per cent (47.7 per cent) from Singapore, Brazil, Argentina; telecommunication equipment: 81.4 per cent (50.0 per cent) from Hong Kong, South Korea, Singapore; electrical machines 'non especially specified' 78.8 per cent (50.0 per cent) from Singapore, South Korea, Hong Kong; textile yarn and thread: 45.6 per cent from South Korea, Brazil, Egypt (54.6 per cent from these countries and Turkey and Pakistan); cotton textiles: 55.6 per cent (43.2 per cent) from India, Hong Kong, Pakistan; non-cotton textiles; 62.6 per cent from India, Bangladesh, Hong Kong (46.5 per cent for these countries and South Korea). Even if some deconcentration has taken place over the years, product and country concentrations are as high as in raw materials'exports.

The industrial countries of the West constitute the chief buyers of manufactured exports from the Third World. In 1970, their share of Third World manufactured exports was 61.7 per cent, however, at the end of the 1970s, it dropped from 63.4 per cent, in 1978, to 56.0 per cent, in 1981. This decline reflected the growing measure of protectionism in the North. In the 1980s, however, the share of the West increased anew, amounting to 69.3 per cent.

At the end of the 1970s, a pattern of differential specialisation emerged for the countries with higher technical capacities. The type of product exported played an important role in determining the degree of dependence on the import markets of the industrial countries. For instance, Latin America and Asia were more dependent on Western industrial markets for simple manufactures (categories 6–8, excluding smelted ores; Latin America: 51.9 per cent, Asia: 65.3 per cent, in 1981) than for machinery and transport equipment (1981: 41.1 per cent, and 56.7 per cent respectively). Backed by protected domestic markets, a few Latin American countries—such as Brazil, Mexico and Argentina—were able to boost the export of their technologically more advanced products, particularly in the sphere of intra-regional trade.

Excluding the OPEC countries (10–11 per cent), the Third World's share of manufactured exports from the developing world declined form 28.1 per cent in 1970, to 21.1 per cent in 1980, recovering again however, to 27.9 per cent in 1981. This recovery was due to a decline in the volume of West European imports.

Here, the Latin American countries (39.3 per cent in 1970, 40 per cent in 1980) were more successful than their Asian counterparts (25.5 per cent in 1970, 19.7 per cent in 1980), with the highest growth being recorded in the exports of machinery and transport equipment to the Third World (1970–1981: 30.8 per cent, p.a.). With regard to those oil-producing countries which have initiated industrialisation programmes, exporters of manufactured goods in other parts of the Third World were deprived of their market shares because these oil producing countries substituted simple consumer goods imports, in particular, with locally produced goods, often turning, in the process, to the industrial West for the most modern technology.

In the 1980s, the debt crises in the South and the liberal US import policies gave rise to a change in this pattern. This was particularly relevant to the US market for machinery and transport equipment, as total US imports of machinery and transport equipment rose at an annual rate of 24 per cent in 1980–87, with imports from Latin America registering 34 per cent (Asia, 22 per cent). European Community markets expanded at 20 per cent, p.a., slightly more rapidly than Japan's corresponding imports, + 19 per cent, p.a. Total US imports of the technologically less demanding 'other manufactures' rose by 17 per cent, p.a., with only minor variations corresponding to the regional origins of production in the Third World (Asia or Latin America). The corresponding growth rates of imports of Japan (+ 9.8 per cent, p.a.) and the European Community (+ 7.8 per cent, p.a.) were less than half of that of the US.

The expansion of South–South trade in manufactures, which between 1970 and 1983 had increased tenfold, came to a halt between 1983 and 1985. The share of developing countries in these countries' manufactured exports declined to 23.3 per cent (17.4 per cent, excluding exports to OPEC countries). Latin American exports of machinery and transport equipment to developing countries declined by 15 per cent, in the period 1980–87, while the exports of other products stagnated, Asian exports of machinery and transport equipment to developing countries increased by 108 per cent in the period 1980–87, reflecting less protectionism. This policy was due to a better debt situation in Asia, as compared to Latin America and Africa.

OPEC imports of machinery and transport equipment from

developing countries (1980–87, + 15 per cent), and other manufactures (+ 27 per cent) indicate that these imports performed better
than the OPEC imports overall. The decline of oil rent made
OPEC countries more price-conscious as was only to be expected.

The disorder in the world economy caused by the increased
protectionism in Western Europe and the debt–induced deflationary policies coupled with high protectionism in Latin America
and Africa, has made manufactured exports from the South more
and more dependent on the import policy of the US. The countries
of Southeast and East Asia, cited as outstanding examples of
success, depend on the markets of the industrial West, especially
the USA, whose absorptive capacity is, however, limited. Since
this is less the case with India and Latin America, this allows for
less reliance on only labour intensive products. As the world economic crisis was met in the South by national measures, the exports
of India and Latin America were the first to suffer. At the same
time, however, because of its excessive dependence on the continuing US preparedness to accept foreign trade deficits, avenues
for the further expansion of Southeast and East Asian exports
were limited. With the exception of Singapore, Hong Kong (two
very special cases), South Korea and Taiwan, manufactured exports
have not led to the clearing of the labour markets in Third World
countries.

In the case of South Korea and Taiwan export–led industrialisation was combined with far-reaching internal reforms (land redistribution), which favoured the development of local markets
and the establishment of high multiplier effects of exports.
However, the *employment effects* deriving from export–oriented
industrialisation are too small to altogether eliminate unemployment in the Third World, although full employment was indeed
achieved in small individual countries, and under special conditions. The free export production zones, which cropped up practically everywhere between 1970 and 1980, generated only one
million jobs worldwide, the linkage effects being extremely small
(70 per cent of local value added is in the form of wages, the rest in
the form of rents and duties, with local intermediate inputs having
no share of the value whatsoever). True, the number of jobs
created by industrial exports, on the whole, might well be greater,
but even fairly optimistic estimates have put the contribution of
manufactured exports to employment in the Third World at

perhaps twenty million, even considering all multiplier effects. This is indeed unsubstantial when compared to the unemployment figures of 350 million for 1980, and 700 million for the year 2000. Even the relocation of the entire manufacturing industry from the OECD–countries (sixty-five million jobs, and no further multiplier effects) could not possibly induce a fundamental change in the labour markets of the Third World.

The estimated figure of twenty million jobs is based on Hong Kong's labour-intensive textile industry (employing a labour force of 234,000 workers in 1977, with exports to the tune of $ 3 million). Price rises due to the devaluation of the dollar, larger shares of imported intermediate goods and machines in the value added in other export-oriented sectors, are overlooked just as much as are the higher labour costs in Latin American countries. All these factors reduce the number of estimated jobs.

Assuming this as the basis, $ 112 billion worth of manufactured goods exported in 1981 would have required nine million workers. But on the basis of the figures for the South Korean textile industry, this value gets reduced, initially, to 6.6 million, and then, to 5.4 million, at price increases of around 5 per cent. Even with higher multiplier effects of between three and four, we still obtain a figure of barely twenty million. (Multiplier = the ratio of the number of workers directly employed in export production to the number of jobs created indirectly through supplies to the export sector and for meeting the demand of those directly employed in exports.)

Hence, the expectation that multiplier effects would be intensified by wage increases in export-oriented enterprises through an expansion in domestic markets is only illusionary. Wage increases for labour can be explained on the basis of growth in productivity only in the event of full employment. Considering the fact that unemployment prevails in most Third World countries, productivity increases, even in the case of manufactured goods, are more likely to lead to price decreases rather than to wage increases. Where low-skilled labour is employed, local scarcity of labour induces a relocation of production to other regions of the same country, or to new countries. Especially in the case of simple products, these precursors of export-oriented industrialisation are being threatened by the emergence of new competitors with even lower wage costs.

Studies exploring the tendency of MNCs to pay relatively high wages in the Third World cannot be cited as proof of rising real wages in the export-oriented industry. For, the 'multis' share of the production of Third World manufactured exports is but small (around 10 per cent in 1966–74). This is true of relatively simple products, such as textiles, as well as of more sophisticated products, other than automobiles and household electronic gadgets. Textiles constitute one-fifth of West German imports from the Third World (1987); in contrast, West German direct investment in textiles worldwide is less than 1 per cent of total direct investment and less than 4 per cent of German direct investment in the South.

In the capital goods industry, the export share of national public and private enterprises is higher than their share of exports in other sectors. The tendency of MNCs to offer above-average conditions of work in the developing countries is counterbalanced by the meagre nature of the MNC–share of export-oriented production, even though as buyers and sellers of these export products in the industrial countries, the MNCs, in the Third World, play off the producers of such goods against each other. The 'sweatshops' or 'world market enterprises' have today ceased to be, and will, in future be even lesser still the domain of the 'multis'.

Even in export-oriented industrialisation, one could expect an increasing measure of state intervention. As opposed to the general line of contention, this would not be introduced to keep labour costs low through the repressive methods of 'bureaucratic-authoritarian' regimes, rather, it would be compelled by the trade restrictions of industrial countries and by the branch-to-branch differences in total factor productivity often referred to as structural heterogeneity. In both cases, rent is appropriated on the basis of monopolistic cost advantages, this being similar to the ways and means of appropriating rent from commodity exports, as described above. Due to the West's allocation of quotas for textile exports from the Third World, the government of Hong Kong is, today, auctioning export licences. Here, high productivity and the low wages paid to textile workers enables the state, with the help of this quota, to raise the unit costs of manufactured exports.

Since an expansion in exports can only be achieved by the production of hitherto unexported products, it becomes necessary to venture into more skill-intensive sectors. This step is, however, not free of serious difficulty. For one, even while the production of simple goods ensures trained labour and improvements in infrastructure, total factor productivity continues to be low in the more skill-intensive branches that are yet to be developed. The result is that products are not competitive. To overcome this, the state can choose to tax those simple products which were hitherto being exported and utilise the revenue to subsidise enterprises investing in the new skill-intensive branches. Singapore is, at present, trying out this method in order to finance the production of more skill-intensive export products.

MULTINATIONAL CORPORATIONS AND THE THIRD WORLD

Until a few years ago, there was a multitude of prognoses, all predicting that, by the close of the century, the entire world production would be controlled by a few large multinational corporations. In contrast, there were only a few who pointed out that since capital export from the industrial countries makes up only a small proportion of capital formation in the Third World, as compared to the years preceding the First World War, the Third World, far from being faced with an excess of foreign capital, has, in reality, to contend with the reluctance of the MNCs to invest capital.

In fact, even the older theory of imperialism grossly overestimated capital export to the South, in the years preceding the First World War, the reason being that it had been too heavily based on the example of Great Britain. However, even in the case of Great Britain, only £ 1786 million out of £ 3763.3 million, were invested in the countries of the South (including South Africa) in the year 1913 (corresponding figures for Germany, France and the USA were 31.1 per cent, 34.4 per cent and 54 per cent respectively). Out of this, 42.4 per cent went to Latin America (£ 756.6 million), particularly to Argentina (£ 319.6 million).

In the years between the two World Wars, capital exports to the Third World stagnated because commodity prices were low. The investment programmes drawn up by the Western colonial powers—especially in the thirties—to promote the development of the colonies, could not offset this trend. It is only since the Second World War that direct investment by the Western industrialised countries in the developing world has once again, been on the rise (The following figures corroborate this point: stock of foreign direct investment in 1967: $ 33 billion; 1971: $ 44 billion; 1975: $ 67 billion; 1980: $ 115 billion; 1985: 131 billion; estimated at current rates of the US $).

The USA continues to be the most important investor. Its share of investment in the Third World was around 45 per cent in the period 1967–71, dropping however to around 40 per cent by 1980. With this, the share of American direct investment (in terms of total volume), in the total direct investment of the four most important industrial countries (USA, Japan, the Federal Republic of Germany and Great Britain), dropped from 74 per cent (1969) to 58 per cent (1979), 55 per cent (1980) and 44 per cent (1985), while West Germany's share increased from 4 per cent to 11 per cent (including large investment sums for Southern Europe), and stood (without investment in Southern Europe) at 9 per cent in 1980, and 6 per cent in 1985. Japan's share rose from 5 per cent (1969) to 20 per cent (1979) and 34 per cent (1985).

The declining share of the USA is, for the most part, to be attributed to nationalisations in the commodity sector (expropriation of crude oil-producing companies), which particularly affected the traditional capital-exporting countries of the USA and Great Britain. The annual growth rate of new investments in the Third World, in the period 1969–1979, amounted to 20.2 per cent for the USA, 20.6 per cent for Great Britain, and 20.6 per cent for Japan. Corresponding values for 1980–85 were: 0.4 per cent, USA; 17.4 per cent, Great Britain; 16.0 per cent, Japan; 20.7 per cent, France; 7.4 per cent, FRG; 7.6 per cent, the Netherlands. In the eighties, direct foreign investment slowly eased off, and its growth was even below Third World exports.

Excluding the period immediately following the nationalisation of the oil companies, the Third World's share of total US foreign investment amounted to just under 25 per cent, 73 per cent of which went to Latin America (1985: 23.4 per cent, of which 54 per cent went to Latin America). In comparison, the Third World's share of Japanese foreign investment is higher and more constant (1969: 56 per cent, 1980: 54 per cent, 1985: 49.5 per cent). The Third World's share of foreign investment of European countries betrays a regressive trend. In the case of West Germany, it fell from 28 per cent in 1966, 24 per cent in 1970, 20 per cent in 1975, 21 per cent in 1979, 19 per cent in 1980 to 13 per cent in 1985 (on excluding the European developing countries), with the threshold country of Brazil individually being a regular recipient of almost a third of the total investment. Brazil now accounts for 43.1 per cent of German investment in the Third World. Even in the case of traditional colonial countries, such as France (1975: 33 per cent; 1979: 27 per cent; 1980: 28 per cent; 1985: 28 per cent), and Great Britain (1971: 26 per cent; 1976: 21 per cent; 1978: 18 per cent; 1985: 19 per cent) the share of the Third World declined.

It is clear that the manufacturing industry now occupies a prominent role in foreign investment in developing countries. Its share (inclusive of the European 'developing countries') of German direct investment amounted to as much as two-thirds in 1979–1985, standing at 70 per cent in 1985. In the case of the USA this share rose from 25 per cent in 1966, to 40 per cent in 1975, this figure falling to 34 per cent in 1980 and 36 per cent in 1985. (A hefty increase in investment in the crude oil sector of the Third World accounts for the slump in 1975–80). At the beginning of the eighties, (1981) 53 per cent of Great Britain's and 57 per cent of Japan's (1980) total capital stock in the Third World was invested in the manufacturing industry. (This surprisingly low figure for Japan is due to the Japanese policy of investing directly in Third World mining).

Today, capital investment in the Third World is of lesser importance for the 'capital employment' of the industrial countries than it used to be prior to World War I. Before 1913, Great Britain, the leading capitalist industrial country, even invested upto 2 per cent of its GNP in the developing countries in particular years. By the end of the seventies, this proportion had sunk to below 1 per cent for all industrial countries, when, in 1913, the proportion of investment in the Third World had risen to one-sixth of Britain's gross fixed capital formation.

In the case of the USA, taking into account even the reinvested profits and value adjustments, capital accumulation through US companies in the South made up no more than a little under 4% of the US gross fixed capital accumulation (1980). Capital flows from the US amounted to 0.45 per cent of US-gross fixed capital accumulation in 1980 and 1.1 per cent in 1986. Similarly, West Germany's net capital transaction to the Third World, by way of direct investment, constituted 0.4 per cent of West German gross capital formation in 1980, with this figure yielding, even negative values in subsequent years.

The contribution of private direct investment to gross capital formation in the Third World is low in even those countries which are widely regarded as important recipient countries, or as being well-integrated into the global economy: 1974–1980 (Figures for 1986 are given in brackets): Brazil, approximately 5 per cent (0.8

per cent); Mexico, approximately 4 per cent (3.3 per cent); Taiwan, 1–2 per cent; Argentina, 0.8–2 per cent (9.1 per cent); Peru 1–6 per cent (6.7 per cent); Indonesia, 3 per cent (1.3 per cent); Korea, approximately 1 per cent in 1975 (1 per cent). Only Singapore registers values of 25–33 per cent (8.3 per cent). Even assuming that capital exports only make up roughly about one-fifth to one-sixth of MNC–investment in the Third World, the rest being financed through reinvested profits and credit raised in the host country itself, the MNC–share of gross fixed capital accumulation, even in economies largely open to them, would amount to less than 10 per cent. This is so for all developing countries with the exception of Brazil, Mexico, Singapore and Indonesia, and even in these cases, predominantly, in the oil sector. The higher shares documented in the literature pertain to the pre–1975 period and include investment in the commodity sectors as well, which are today, to a large extent, nationalised. In 1986, in addition to Singapore and Argentina, high shares were recorded in Columbia (12.6 per cent), Malaysia (7.7 per cent), and Tunisia (8.5 per cent).

The share of foreign companies in total sales appears to be declining in some important capital-importing countries: In Brazil, for instance, the share of the MNCs in the electronic industry fell from 65 per cent to 45 per cent (1976–79); in the case of plastic products, it dropped from 88 per cent to 31 per cent; in medicines, from 75 per cent to 70 per cent, and for textiles, from 14 per cent to 13 per cent. (Due to the increasing complexity of joint ventures, there is no reliable data for the 1980s).

Even for Latin America, *the share of foreign companies in industrial employment* is estimated at a mere 10–11 per cent (approximately). With the exception of Singapore, their contribution to employment in other regions is even more insignificant. This is borne out by the fact that direct investment in the Third World is regionally concentrated in Latin America. Of the $ 85 billion invested in 1978 (inclusive of the European developing countries), $ 42 billion, or just under 50 per cent, was invested *in only thirteen countries* in the following order of precedence: Brazil, Mexico, Indonesia, the Bermudas, Venezuela, Argentina, Panama, Malaysia, India, the Dutch Antilles, the Bahamas, Hong Kong. 82 per cent of the US investment in the Third World manufacturing industry is concentrated in Latin America in the period 1970–1981 (54 per cent in 1985). For the Federal Republic of Germany, Latin America accounted for 60 per cent in 1978, and 76 per cent in 1985 (after excluding the European developing countries). Again, in the 1970s, 43 per cent of Great Britain's investment in the manufacturing industry of the South went to Latin America (1981: 34 per cent).

Thus, it is not the export-oriented industries of finished goods in Asia that constitute the main areas of investment in the manufacturing industry, rather investment mainly takes place in countries like Brazil, Mexico, and Argentina, which have extensive protected domestic markets. In fact, Asia's share of direct investments in the manufacturing industry of the South amounted to 36.3 per cent in the case of Japan (1981), 33.5 per cent, in the case of Great Britain (1981), 43 per cent for the USA (1985), and 11 per cent in the case of the Federal Republic of Germany (1985) (excluding the non-Europeon developing countries).

Direct investment by the MNCs tends to concentrate more on the technology-intensive branches of the manufacturing industry. Electronic goods (based on simple technologies) received, in 1980, 40 per cent (1985: 39 per cent) of US foreign investment in Asia. 36 per cent (1981) of British direct investment in Latin America went to the food-processing industry, while typical products of export-oriented industrialisation, like textiles, amounted to 5 per cent (1981) of British foreign investment. In comparison, Japanese direct investment in Asia's manufacturing industry (1981: $ 4.75 billion) is, in absolute terms, higher than that in Latin America ($ 2.78 billion). One-third of this is accounted for by higher investments in the textile industry, a further one-sixth each is attributable to metal processing and electrical products, and the rest, almost totally, to higher investment in other consumer goods industries (toys, sports gear).

Thus, the direct investment of MNCs in the South is only partially conditioned by the new international division of labour. MNCs enter such branches for which technical know-how is essential, and whose level of technology is higher than that of the frontline branches of export-oriented industrialisation. Aside from the tax havens and the refineries of small countries, MNCs sink their direct investments in populous countries in which a certain domestic market exists.

Primarily, the MNCs do not invest in those branches of the Third World which enjoy comparative cost advantages on the basis of the availability of cheap labour. True, the companies, more often than not, cite the payment of low wages as a motivation for direct investment, but, in actuality, this is only one of the motivations, the primary one being the protection of markets. It is not so much the comparative cost advantages of the host countries which is a factor of importance for the foreign investments of Western companies, but also the cost advantages vis-a-vis other national enterprises in Third World countries having ·markets with relatively high consumptive capacities that plays a major role in motivating direct investment. Such company-specific cost advantages can only be explained on the basis of technological leads which, in turn, derive from a monopolistic control over technology.

Therefore, the MNCs have to also necessarily invest modern technology within the framework of foreign investment, so as to capitalise on their cost advantage. Besides, due to the low level of foreign activities, there is often little incentive to employ technology which is better adapted to factor costs in production. The MNCs' concentration on *durable consumer goods* for high-income recipients, on high proportions of imported technology and imported intermediate inputs in the production sites of MNCs in the Third World, have—despite all efforts at adjustment on the part of the enterprises—proved to be rational for industrial operation. The same is true of the strategy of paying relatively *high wages*, as this enables the company to gain the backing of its personnel, and thus, to insulate itself from political intervention.

This is countered by the argument that MNCs show a greater propensity to export than Third World national enterprises. However, this lead disappears if the branch-to-branch divergences in this export propensity are taken into account. Typically, MNC–subsidiaries are well represented in the export of durable consumer goods (including automobiles), whereas technology export, in the narrower sense of the word (turnkey projects, ships, machines) reveals a disproportionately large representation of national enterprises in the more advanced developing countries.

The relationship between foreign investment and technological advantages poses obstacles to economic growth, in the conditions that prevail in underdeveloped countries. The technology adopted in sectors which are of interest to foreign investors creates relatively few jobs. The market for the selected products is very restricted owing to the inequitable distribution of income that prevails right from the outset. As a result of low income effects (extremely low level of employment), there is only a small expansion in markets for foreign investors. *Monopolistic practices*, employed to increase sales by crowding out indigenous producers, become inevitable. Because of the large financial reserves of the parent-companies, these monopolistic practices can be implemented over a period of time—even by adopting the strategy of selling at a loss—so much so that, often, political reactions are provoked. Ultimately, only so-called 'marginal suppliers' remain in the fray, as proof of surviving competition.

The restricted market for goods of greater technological sophistication makes the reinvestment of accumulated profits difficult. Many Third World governments flay the MNCs for the negative nature of their financial contribution to the developing countries. With the relatively small capital inflows from abroad, small production capacities can be set up, or local units bought up and modernised. Often, the units are so small (miniaturized) that their unit costs of production are too high for export. The MNCs also invest in small markets, which they perceive as lucrative precisely because others have already invested in them (the practice of follow-the-leader). Owing to restricted growth opportunities, profits realised after the initial build-up phase are 'retransferred', i.e., are remitted back to parent companies, or, perhaps, to MNC–subsidiaries in tax havens.

If the government of the host country was to try to control such return remittances, the subsidiaries could resort to a policy of '*transfer pricing*' while trading with foreign subsidiaries of the parent company. Due to the company-specific nature of technologies, there are often no fixed world market prices for import and export goods, to the extent that these constitute preliminary and intermediate products in a production process which is decentralised all over the world. Low export prices, or high prices for products supplied by other MNC–subsidiaries favour such a strategy of *profit transfer*, thereby undermining both the exchange control measures as well as the taxing avenues of the governments of the host country.

Impediments to subsequent growth result from the tendency of the MNCs to specialise in goods catering to the demand of the high-income groups of the Third World, thus restricting growth opportunities. MNCs are, therefore, regarded as *positive–negative*. In the initial phase, they promote growth. But as soon as the absorptive capacity of the high-income markets dries up, they become growth-impeding. There is a positive correlation between the level of annual investment (i.e., new investment) and the growth rate, whereas in the case of the quantity of capital accumulated, the correlation to the growth rate is negative. On these grounds it is contended that the investment activity of MNCs ultimately leads to an impasse.

Hence, the thrust of the MNC–policies of Third World governments is two-pronged: These governments, firstly, try to use the MNCs to bring foreign technology into their respective countries under the most favourable conditions and, subsequently, try to retain the profits of the MNCs for reinvestment within the country.

Practically all Third World countries seek the cooperation of MNCs, either as suppliers of technology or, as direct investors. While buying technology, the governments have to bear the costs. However, they often receive large credits from banks in the home country of their partners. They also obtain assurances that a portion of the product will be bought. Since overtly restrictive clauses, such as those prohibiting the sale of products manufactured in acquired plants on the world market, or in certain external markets, have diminished under the influence of multinational organisations since the sixties, there has been a growing tendency to supply technology and to fulfil the commitments made regarding the training of the prospective employees of the host country in such a restricted manner that the country concerned cannot possibly develop further in future with the technology purchased.

Where the governments of the Third World have followed a policy of encouraging direct investment, they have granted cheap land, infrastructural benefits and tax privileges, in the hope of taxing the foreign company at some later date. Since the MNCs are quite aware of this danger, they prefer stepping into countries whose governments they feel would not resort to such measures, in other words, pro-Western governments which are known to be stable. The indicators for stability involve factors such as the repressive capacity of the regime and the weakness or strength of the labour movement. Often, the governments of the South point to the weakness of their trade unions, using this as a means to draw investment from abroad. But even pro-Western governments (as in Brazil, Mexico) try to exert control over the subsidiaries of foreign companies installed in their countries as soon as the balance of payment pressures described above make themselves felt.

In any case, the belief that investments in the Third World are put to risk by political uncertainties often leads to a cost calculation on the part of investors, whereby the gross sum invested has to be amortised after a few years, at times within a period of three years. This presupposes high rates of profit at the outset. Therefore, investments are made only when opportunities for profit are extremely great. Every additional profit made after the period taken into consideration—provided the governments of the host countries do not resort to the expected control measures after this period—is an added gift from the host country.

Transborder relations between foreign subsidiaries are seen to be a point at which governments may intervene in order to control the subsidiaries of foreign companies operating within their respective territories. If the import rights of the subsidiaries are fixed as a percentage of their exports, and this—while pointing to the deterioration in the balance of payment position—increasingly proves to the disadvantage of these subsidiaries, the following pattern is set into motion for the latter: If high import prices or low export prices are billed with the remaining sectors of the parent company, the volume of importable goods falls. If the company is still viable, it has to shift over to the local production of intermediate goods, as a result of which there is greater linkage with local producers. This can even lead to the subsidiaries of foreign countries successfully calling upon their foreign suppliers to produce the intermediate and capital goods concerned in the host country. Similarly, linking up the amount of remittable profit to the balance between the export revenue and import costs of the subsidiary can result in the latter either increasing its exports, relying to a greater extent on local suppliers, or investing its profits within the country in production branches other than those it had hitherto operated.

In each case, what transpires is a struggle for rent in a structurally heterogeneous economy. Production projected at the outset yields an above-average rate of profit, although there are no investment avenues within the country which could possibly yield average profits by international standards. On an overall basis, the foreign subsidiaries still manage to secure average profit rates, even when the costs of intermediate inputs rise due to import restrictions, or when investments have to be sunk in production branches which only yield below-average profit rates, or when prices on the world market for additional exports are below the average unit costs, but above the marginal costs. Countries with large domestic markets enjoy greater bargaining power because, in their case, losses through diversification of production, reliance on more expensive local suppliers, or the increase in the volume of exports in relation to profits secured from hitherto operational production lines are smaller than in countries with small domestic markets. This mechanism can, however, be put to use even by the small countries.

The possibilities open to the governments of Third World countries to bring the foreign subsidiaries of Western companies under control have often been underestimated. The small countries–big companies thesis measured the 'smallness' of the country on the basis of its GNP, and the 'largeness' of the company on the basis of its turnover. This basis of measurement is , however, wrong. Large oil companies have high turnovers because the prime cost of crude (government selling, or taxing by the oil-producing country) is high. Large companies in the manufacturing industry are dependent on a number of suppliers. Therefore, the reference figure should be derived on the basis of the value added of the companies measured against the GNP of the developing countries.

The increasing role of national sovereignty is reflected in the series of nationalisations in the developing countries, particularly after 1973. By 1975, as much as 75 per cent of the raw material investment of the USA in the Third World was nationalised. Between 1960 and 1975, the UN recorded as many as 1369 nationalisations in the Third World, and that too, in seventy-one countries, of which twenty-six countries had nationalised more than ten companies each. Two hundred and twenty subsidiaries of foreign companies engaged in oil production, eighty engaged in mining, and two hundred and seventy-two in agriculture, were nationalised. By comparison, the manufacturing industry was subject to only a relatively small number of nationalisations (221), most of which were the direct outcome of the process of decolonisation in Africa. Outside Africa, however, the manufacturing industry witnessed as many as one hundred nationalisations in 1960–1976, the period 1970–1976 alone accounting for as many as sixty, of which forty-nine took place in 'stable' Latin America.

These nationalisations did not by any means lead to 'prompt, appropriate and full compensation', as demanded by the companies affected. In the raw material sector, countries such as Algeria and Iraq presented companies with additional tax demands based on previous disputes, these claims being fixed at a level corresponding to the level of compensation agreed upon. In what are considered to be pro-West countries, Western companies had to rest content with the book value of their plants being adjusted against the rate of inflation for capital goods. With this, accelerated depreciations, which were previously undertaken with the objective of reducing profits (in other words, latent reserves in capital assets), were lost.

In the manufacturing sector, the payment of compensation hinged, to a large extent, on the willingness and ability of the company to enter into further cooperation. In cases where the expropriating country needed the marketing avenues, or the technical assistance of the parent company, and was offered a reasonable regulatory framework towards this end by the latter, compensation was higher than in other cases. The more company-specific the technology, and the more company-specific the markets, the greater was the bargaining power of the company. But due to severe competition prevailing in world capital export, the developing country could always find a partner, thus diminishing the significance of the threat of the technological reliance of the subsidiary on its parent company. Besides, in the commodity sector it is impossible to control the markets through company-specific technologies and production norms (for example, specifications for individual components).

An awareness of the growing importance of state sovereignty lies at the basis of the policy adopted by the MNCs in their interaction with Third World governments. Let us first look at the *commodity sector*, which is experiencing marginalisation in the Third World. Contrary to popular belief, what looms ahead as a potential threat is not the depletion of raw material reserves, but a curtailment of raw material exploration in the Third World. By 1980, there were 40,000 oil wells in Africa, 100,000 in Latin America as compared to 2.2 million in the USA. Between 1961 and 1975, the Third World share of investment in world raw material exploration (other than in the crude oil sector) declined from 57 per cent to 15 per cent. Western companies continue to be interested in commodity supplies from the Third World, though they are no longer willing to have a stake in the risk capital. Where West German companies have direct equity participation in Third World countries (for example, Liberia), they finance the investments of their affiliates through credit raised from (West German) shareholders rather than through risk capital. If the affiliate is nationalised, the host country is not required to pay compensation but has to repay its debts. An often adopted ploy that ensures even greater security is one which restricts the role of the company to that of a mere supplier of technology who renders services against payment from the developing country, these services not being financed by the company itself but, as far as possible, by banks not associated with the company in any way.

Meanwhile, the governments of the South are no longer willing to assume the full burden of the technical risks themselves (for example, uncertainty of striking raw material). In fact, extremely complicated forms of contracts between the two parties are often drafted, these even stipulating that Western partners bear part of the technical risks involved in raw material exploration, allowing them, however, to have primacy in payment after the commencement of production in order to safeguard the company against political risks.

In the *manufacturing sector*, Western companies are increasingly on the lookout for local partners in production. To the extent to which this is possible, production runs are split up and distributed on a regional basis. Where production is split up into individual steps, the nationalisation of a company would provide the host country with only those products which the parent company would find useful. Where the very same production steps are spread out over an entire region, a fall in the production in one country can easily be offset by increasing production in the other countries. The ruling elites of the Third World are granted equity participation in an attempt to get them interested in the well-being of the company concerned, though this does not actually give them an effective voice in company affairs since further production depends on the supply of technology.

The 'positive' and 'negative' roles played simultaneously by MNC–subsidiaries is a consequence of prevailing income distribution and the company-specific cost advantages of the MNCs in the capital-intensive production of durable consumer goods for restricted markets. Since employment-generating effects are too small to create mass markets, which would, in turn, facilitate the development of new production branches, adjustment opportunities are further restricted by the exhaustion of demand from high income groups, with the effect that there is increasing pressure to remit profits. At the same time, there is a growing tendency on the part of the governments to interfere in the business activities of the companies.

By investing in the Third World, the MNCs are not 'making a wager on the development of the host country' (Emmanuel). Far from being too strong, they are, on the other hand, too weak to create the requisite conditions for self-sustaining growth. The number of jobs generated is too small to create a mass demand, by changing the structure of labour markets. The apparently essential 'capitalistic' market proves to be their nemesis. They find a greater degree of security with governments which are more sceptical in their attitudes towards social reform in favour of the lower classes. Companies always have a business-oriented perception of the economy which often makes them incapable of understanding that their growth—even in their home countries—depends on the increase in mass demand.

While negotiating on the distribution of surplus profit, the MNCs become partners of Third World State–classes, whom they help finance. Here, by restricting themselves to entrepreneurial goals in keeping with the dictates of social desirability—for whoever wanted to assign them the responsibility for social policies?—the MNCs are led into close cooperation with those segments of the State–class averse to reform, and to evolve a strategy of creating technological dependency which renders social structural change difficult.

PROBLEMS OF TECHNOLOGY TRANSFER

The industrialised countries of the West accounted for 98 per cent of the expenditure towards research and development (excluding the COMECON countries), the Third World by contrast made up a mere 2 per cent at the end of the 1970s. Even now, correlation remains much the same, although the share of the expenditure on research and development in the GNP has been on the increase in the newly industrialising countries. It goes without saying that corresponding to this fact, the Third World's share of new patents is exceedingly low. Of course, this observation is not to suggest that the countries of the Third World invent afresh all the technological innovations of the West, for *the purchase of technology is cost-saving*. At the same time it must be noted that this *prevents the development of an indigenous technological base*. The share of the Third World in world production of non-electrical machinery, the major branch of equipment production, has declined between 1975 (4.8 per cent) and 1985 (4.3 per cent), with the share of this branch in the total manufacturing production of the Third World also declining from 1975 (5.0 per cent) to 1985 (4.6 per cent). At present, the share is about one-third of the corresponding share for developed market economies (1985: 12.7 per cent). The rate of growth of this branch had been 10.9 per cent p.a. through 1965–75 in the Third World, but it has declined to 1.9 per cent through 1975–85.

Technology development and production are labour-intensive and depend not only on the research efforts of academically proven specialists but also on the knowledge and experience of the engineers and technical experts, who are given further training in machine construction. Productivity increases with the use of new machinery, therefore, provides the base for the mass of innovation.

Let us suppose that a producer holds monopoly rights for a new machine whose employment would curtail the demand for labour and intermediate inputs. He could raise the price of this machine to the sum of the price of the old machine and economies of other cost factors. However, it has been found that production costs of new machines do not rise on the same scale: The history of the Western industrialised countries, since the close of the nineteenth century, has revealed that the ratio of the value of total production to the value of machinery—capital productivity—has changed only to a small extent. It can be proved that this relative stability of capital productivity is essential to capitalism.

If the producer of machinery can secure his monopoly price, then his factor productivity and the rate of profit will be higher than that of the rest of the economy. The mechanism of competition in a capitalistic economy corrects this difference because competition between the various producers of machinery compels these to reduce their prices to the level of production costs (including an average rate of interest on capital). Production costs will then decrease even in those sectors which use the machinery (without developing it). A portion of the technical progress achieved will be absorbed in increasing the productivity of employers of new technology. Further increases in productivity, however, depend on the level of competence attained in machine-building.

By importing capital goods, the Third World initially acquires only the capacity to use, but not to produce, machinery. The more capital-intensive a method of production, the greater the amount of work needed as input before the machine can be employed and, hence, fewer the learning opportunities for the employer. Thus, the import of capital-intensive technologies reduces the Third World's learning opportunities where the application of imported technologies is concerned. *Differences in factor productivities between economies at various stages of development are most marked in the area of technology production.* At exchange rates reflecting the difference in the *average* productivity of two economies, the production of modern equipment goods appears to be unprofitable in the lesser developed economy.

Less developed economies can break the impasse of technological dependency only by building up an indigenous technological base through the local production of machinery, even if this pushes up costs temporarily. Since this production has to initially draw on locally available skills, only simple machinery can be produced at the outset. A prerequisite for the application of such production technologies is that corresponding technologies are in use in the remaining branches of production. However, learning does not necessitate the local production of all technologies but of only a certain portion large enough to ensure that the number of workers engaged in machine production suffices for the 'assimilation' of imported technologies.

Certain social and political mechanisms operating in the under-developed countries render the production and application of local technologies difficult. The higher quality demands of the rich foster the import of technology. Where capital-intensive technologies are employed, wage costs play a less significant role even though skilled labour is scarce. Contradictions inherent in import-substituting industrialisation surface. Technology imports are necessitated to satisfy the demand for luxury items, favouring, in the process, an inequitable distribution of income which, in turn, promotes technology import once again.

The State–class, for the most part, has little technical competence. The promotion of local technology production would entail that it relinquish its position of preponderance in the society to skilled workers and engineers. Modern technology enables managers to have better control over labour since machines set the rhythm of work. Simple, locally produced turning lathes would be less credible in demonstrating the process of 'catching-up' with the industrial countries, than would ultra-modern steel works or power stations, which are the objects of prestige. Consequently, technicians and engineers show a marked preference for modern technology, even in production steps for which simpler and more labour-intensive methods would be more efficient economically, due to lower labour costs.

Further, import of modern technology allows room for bribery and corruption: For the entrepreneur, where machinery is concerned, the reliability of, and the production volumes attainable by the machines are factors which are more important than the price. As a result, a higher price can be negotiated during purchase by claiming that the machine possesses these characteristics, thereby leaving leeway for the payment of bribes to the managers of companies in the developing country.

The reliance on imported technology gives rise to financial dependence precisely at such times when the Third World countries are making efforts to industrialise. Increased investment will lead to a growth in imports, if no local capital goods production exists. An increase in the level of investment in an underdeveloped country will not lead to greater financial dependence only in those cases where an increasing volume of capital goods is being produced within the country.

In reality, over the last eighteen years, capital goods imports of the developing countries have actually risen more rapidly than their total imports. The share of capital goods (SITC 7 excluding automobiles) in Third World imports (excluding fuel) accounted for 34.3 per cent in 1970, 36.9 per cent in 1980 and 36.9 per cent in 1987; excluding the OPEC countries : 37.2 per cent, 36 per cent and 37.5 per cent. At the same time, the share of industrial consumer goods (SITC 6+8 excluding 68 . 1970, 28.3 per cent; 1980, 28.3 per cent; 1987, 27.4 per cent; excluding the OPEC countries : 26.8 per cent, 26.7 per cent) in imports (excluding fuel) did not fall.

The growth in capital goods imports did not bring about a corresponding increase in production. The average annual rate of growth of the capital goods imports of the developing market economies, adjusted to the US price index for capital goods, was approximately 15 per cent p.a. for the period 1970–1979 (excluding the OPEC-countries: 10.3 per cent). In comparison, the growth rates for production were considerably lower: The manufacturing industry in middle-income countries, to which the mass of the capital goods exports went, recorded a growth rate of 6.6 per cent p.a., whereas this figure was 3.6 per cent for lower income countries (excluding India and China). Growth in GNP, agricultural production and the service sector was considerably slower.

The 1980s were characterised by declining real capital goods imports (machinery and transport equipment). Even in nominal terms, the import of capital goods into Africa declined, in 1987, to 70 per cent of its 1980 level; in Middle Eastern countries, to 81 per cent; while Latin America recorded a stagnation. These exports to other Asian countries, grew by 82 per cent in nominal terms and 38 per cent in real terms, based on the price index for equipment goods. Manufacturing production continued to rise at appreciable rates in India (+ 8.2 per cent p.a.) and China (+ 12.6 per cent p.a.) during 1980–86, and by 4.8 per cent in the other low income countries, covering however wide differences (subsaharan Africa + 0.3 per cent). The growth rate in the middle-income countries was at a low 2.5 per cent due to very low rates (and even negative ones) in Latin America, especially in the more advanced countries (Mexico 0 per cent, Argentina 0.4 per cent, Chile − 0.2 per cent, Brazil + 1.2 per cent), whereas Asian growth rates were appreciable even in the second generation of export-oriented industrialising countries (Malaysia, Thailand, Indonesia). This performance in the crisis seems to indicate that the degree of dependence on imported technology before the crisis of the 1980s, had not been inevitable.

Alongside capital goods imports, new modes of technology transfer are becoming increasingly important since the 1970s. In the case of some industrially more advanced countries, payments for licences make up as much as upto 5 per cent of export earnings (Mexico: 1976, 5.2 per cent; Argentina: 1979, 4.2 per cent; Brazil: 1977, 3.1 per cent). Additional costs are contained in the profits made by the MNCs: In keeping with the framework of the new modes of cooperation with local partners, these MNCs 'pay' their share of equity in a joint venture, not in the form of cash (foreign exchange), but in the form of technology (blue prints, documentations). This transfer of technical documentations, earns them their equity share, costs them practically nothing and, on the other hand, entitles them to a portion of the profit made by joint ventures in the Third World. Industrialisation without local technology production has proved a burden on the trade balance and the balance of payment, apart from exacerbating indebtedness because growth in industrial production did not keep pace with the imports of capital goods.

THIRD WORLD INDEBTEDNESS

Until the outbreak of the debt crisis, as per the rather cautious figures of the OECD, the volume of Third World debt has increased from $ 90 to 627 billion for the period 1970–1981 (excluding the OPEC countries: from $ 45 to 402 billion), debt service (principal and interest) having gone up from $ 9.3 to 124.4 billion (excluding the OPEC countries from $ 8 to 92 billion). Bank loans had become, in the 1970s the most important source of finance for the developing countries, superseding even the direct investments of the MNCs and the official development aid programmes of the industrial countries in terms of importance. With this, a growing proportion of credit was granted at prevailing market rates, and not on concessional terms, as was the case with official development assistance. This factor, combined with the increase in interest rates on Western capital markets, gave rise to a situation in which the higher-income countries were, and still are today, heavily in debt and able to meet a mere 9 per cent of their financial requirements through development aid. The debt crisis (the fear of devaluation), in turn, leads to the flight of private capital from the developing countries involved (1980–1982: $ 61 billion).

The indebtedness of Third World countries was only partially attributable to their poverty. Measured in terms of their GNP, low-income countries are just as heavily indebted as middle-income countries, but measured in terms of their export earnings, they are even more heavily indebted. However, their share of total Third World debt (excluding that of the OPEC countries) is small (21 per cent in 1982).

TABLE 7

Third World Debt in 1980 (in billions of $)

Debt	Population (in millions)	GNP (in billions of $)	Exports (in billions of $)	Debt Service (in billions of $)	Debt			Debt Service			Growth in Debt	
					per capita ($)	as a percentage of GNP	as a % of exports	per capita ($)	as a % of GNP	as a % of exports	1971–80 %	1980–82 %
Low income countries	1298	370	48	7.9	66	23	179	6.1	2.1	16.4	511	27.9
Least developed countries	276	67	8	1.2	69	28	238	4.3	1.7	15.0	–	–
Middle-income countries	331	384	135	16.8	323	28	79	47.2	4.3	12.4	328	34.5
Newly Industrialising countries	356	1010	225	40.5	539	19	85	113.7	4.0	18.1	500	38.5
OPEC	339	606	305	27.7	233	13	26	81.7	4.6	9.1	426	34.5

TABLE 8

Net Financing Flows to the Third World (billions of $)

	1970	1971	1972	1973	1974	1975	1976	1977	1978	1979	1980	1981	1982	1983	1984	1985	1986	1987
Net resource flows (excluding short term lending)	19.0	21.2	23.4	32.2	36.2	54.4	58.2	63.8	83.3	85.6	102.0	115.7	101.3	120.1	91.6	71.8	87.7	91.9
Concessional aid	8.1	9.4	10.1	12.4	16.5	20.9	19.7	20.4	27.2	30.6	37.8	36.9	34.0	33.9	35.0	37.4	44.3	48.4
Concessional aid from Western industrial countries and multilateral agencies, excluding OPEC	6.7	7.7	8.0	9.1	10.9	13.5	14.0	19.7	18.2	21.9	25.7	26.0	25.8	26.0	27.6	29.4	35.9	n.a.
Foreign Direct Investment	3.7	3.3	4.2	4.7	1.9	11.5	8.6	9.6	11.8	13.4	10.2	17.1	12.7	9.3	11.5	7.5	11.8	20.2
Bank Loans	5.4	6.3	6.7	11.4	12.7	16.8	23.4	27.8	35.8	31.3	29.0	30.0	22.6	61.7	22.4	25.6	9.0	0.6

In each country group (see Table 7), 50 per cent of the debts were accounted for by just a handful of countries (1980). Between them Algeria, Indonesia and Venezuela shared $ 48.5 billion of the $ 79 billion debt of the OPEC. Within the group of newly industrialising countries, the South European 'developing countries' were also represented as carrying a debt burden of $ 43.6 billion. Of the remaining $ 148.4 billion, Brazil and Mexico accounted for $ 100.4 billion. Within the group of seventy-three middle-income countries, one-tenth of the countries—Turkey, Chile, Philippines, Israel, Morocco, Colombia and Thailand—together bore 53.7 per cent of the debt. Amongst the sixty-one low-income countries with a total debt of $ 86 billion, India, Egypt, Pakistan, Zaire and Bangladesh alone made up 56 per cent.

The heavily indebted low-income countries were severely hit both by the rise in fuel prices as well as by the regressive trends in export earnings. However, since 1975, their debt had been increasing at a rate which was clearly below average . The banks' share of debt was low. Almost all the heavily indebted countries of the middle-income groups (with the exception of Chile and Peru) and the newly industrialising countries, and even Egypt, revealed an extremely high rate of growth in investment for the period 1970–79 (Egypt 21.5 per cent, Morocco 15 per cent, Korea 14.9 per cent, Ivory Coast 13.8 per cent, Hong Kong 12.5 per cent, Tunisia 11.4 per cent, Philippines 10.6 per cent, Malaysia 10.3 per cent, Turkey 10.1 per cent, Brazil 10.1 per cent). In the case of Brazil, energy costs have also to be taken into account. Apart from the high rate of growth in public consumption, the contradictions inherent in import-substituting industrialisation are, once again, revealed in the case of Mexico and Argentina.

Excepting the case of the low-income countries, the indebtedness of the Third World is the outcome of efforts to develop industry, of an 'indebted industrialisation'. The increase in debt was attributable to high rates of growth in investment coupled with a steady rise in the rising share of capital goods in the imports of these countries, this despite the increase in fuel prices. Only the more successful among the exporters of manufactured goods, namely, some Southeast and East Asian countries, were able to restrict debt service, payment of principal and interest as a percentage of export earnings, to below 20 per cent through a rapid increase in their exports. Brazil utilised 58 per cent, p.a. of its export earnings for debt service, Mexico 60 per cent and the two most heavily indebted OPEC countries Algeria and Venezuela, 26 per cent and 27 per cent, respectively.

The *state* in the Third World is *the chief promoter of indebted industrialisation*. Only 8 per cent of the Eurocredit taken by the countries of the Third World went to private parties, in contrast, 54 per cent went to the public sector and 34 per cent to governments. Low capital costs, resulting from a slump in investment in the industrial countries, encouraged a good number of Third World governments to try and step up industrialisation by importing capital goods from the West. The expansion of the public sector served as a means towards this end. To some extent, considerable gains in production were achieved. In some countries like Malaysia, Brazil, Korea, Singapore and Thailand, the rate of growth in manufacturing production exceeded that of investment. In all other cases the growth rates of production were substantially lower; thus capital productivity in these countries declined with increasing investment efforts.

Where these countries imitated the strategy of manufactured exports for which there was a great demand, their entry into the market with their products coincided with the rise in protectionism in the industrial countries. With the introduction of quotas restricting export opportunities, newcomers are at a special disadvantage for they cannot lay claims by pointing to market shares already secured.

Thus, the debt problem of the developing countries is on three counts, the outcome of the recession in the industrial countries of the West. With the absence of growth and full employment in the West, the chances of payments for capital goods imports with manufactured exports are extremely slim. Where the governments of the West are themselves faced with empty treasuries, development aid ceases to increase in real terms. The governments of the West fight recession by restricting the money supply, thereby giving rise to high interest rates as is the case today. The debt crisis clearly reveals that, instead of building up their own industrial base, the developing countries have propped up their industrial development not only on loans, but also on technology bought on credit, a policy prompted by certain politico-social reasons.

The debt situation, as described for the early 1980s, has, since then, worsened dramatically. Due to recession and high interest rates, overall debt has increased to $ 1,240 billion in 1988 and debt service to $ 178 billion, due, in part, to the statistical coverage of short-term debt since 1982 (Revised total debt in 1982: $ 835 billion). The development of the debt according to new groupings made by OECD shows that the expansion of the debt could be challenged in the case of upper middle-income countries (1982–88 + 25 per cent), but not in the case of the low middle-income countries (+ 78 per cent) and the low-income countries (+ 111 per cent).

With respect to the upper middle-income countries, debt expansion was due to some successful export-oriented industrialising countries (Taiwan, Malaysia, Hong Kong, South Korea: 25.3 per cent of the increase in total debt): the cautious expansion of the debt in the case of Brazil (+ 29 per cent), Mexico (+ 24 per cent), and Argentina (+ 35 per cent); the three countries representing 50.3 per cent of the debt increase of the group; and debt increases of Algeria (+ 38 per cent), Iraq (+ 206 per cent), Israel (+ 28.3 per cent) and Chile (+ 27 per cent), these countries representing another 23.5 per cent of the debt increase of the group.

In the low middle-income countries, some $ 13 billion of the total increase of $ 72 billion is attributable to the socialist countries, especially Cuba, Mongolia, and Nicaragua, they being indebted to other socialist countries. There are nine countries among the twenty-six non-socialist countries which account for 95 per cent of the total increase, two of which (Turkey and Thailand) account for 53 per cent of the increase in debt of the non-socialist, low middle-income countries. Debt increase in these cases is due to the attempt to build up export–oriented industries.

Among the seventy-seven members of the group of low-income countries, seven countries (Indonesia, India, Egypt, Nigeria, Philippines, Pakistan, Bangladesh and Zaire) account for 55 per cent of the total debt increase of the group, but their share has been declining (1982: 66 per cent), even if heavily borrowing China is excluded (share of the seven countries in total debt of the group excluding China: 68 per cent in 1982, 60 in 1988).

It was, therefore, the smaller countries which had to increase their debt even more than the average of the group. The debt crisis, which started as a growth-induced disequilibrium of the balance of trade and the balance of payment of the more advanced countries, turns out to be most detrimental for those economies of the South which are small and poor, and which have difficulty in adapting themselves.

4

A 'New International Economic Order' or A 'New Development Policy'?

THE PROGRESS TOWARDS A NEW INTERNATIONAL ECONOMIC ORDER

The international economic order set up at the close of World War II reflects the US policy to be one which aims at averting yet another world economic recession. This order turned away from the concept of economic nationalism which came to be widespread in Europe in the period between the two World Wars. Ever since 1935, the USA has been trying to ease trade barriers through a policy of bilateral trade agreements (the 'most-favoured nation' clause). Following the first great success (1938: Anglo–American trade agreement wherein Great Britain agrees to do away with preferential tariffs within its Empire), this policy continued to be consistently pursued by the US at the various conferences convened by the Western Allies throughout the Second World War. This led to the establishment of the IMF and the GATT in 1947.

The IMF is a common bank of all the Western countries which is funded through the subscriptions of its members. The Fund can use this capital to grant loans on fixed terms to those of its member countries which are faced with an adverse balance of payment position. In the face of constantly recurring difficulties in the balance of payment, member countries could, henceforth, use the IMF as a support base to sustain free trade. If a country's balance of payment deficit were to grow, then the credit lines from the

IMF, which would normally be extended to it automatically, or on favourable terms, would dry up. Further credit can be granted if the country concerned introduces measures which restore its international competitiveness. Here, the IMF can lay down certain conditions, as it has done in innumerable cases (currency devaluation, the curtailment of public spending).

For the developing countries, such conditions constitute a grave interference in their economic policies. Due to the low degree of flexibility in their economies, devaluation induces price increases for important imports without effecting a rise of equal magnitude, either in local production, or in export earnings. The curtailment of public expenditure often necessarily means forfeiting investment projects, or the subsidisation of the essential commodities of the urban population. In several cases, the conditions imposed were so drastic that they sparked off political unrest and had to be revoked, at least in part.

The GATT has been the scene of differences of opinion between the industrial countries. Unlike the USA, which expected full employment to result from the mere liberalisation of world trade, Great Britain, influenced by Keynesian thought, stood for the establishment of an international trade organisation whose members would be committed to strive for full employment, and which, at the same time, would adopt measures to help countries with unemployment regain full employment. However Great Britain's economic weakness in the immediate post-war years permitted the USA to push ahead with its proposals.

This system was complemented by the World Bank, which was to grant credit on prevailing market terms for projects which appeared to be of particular urgency (especially for the reconstruction of war-ravaged Europe). A complementary measure was the elevation of the dollar to the status of a reserve currency. With its large gold reserves, the USA was in a position to always remain committed to redeem dollars into gold at a fixed rate. The dollar rate of all other currencies was fixed individually at a particular exchange rate to the dollar. The central banks of all the other countries were committed to defend this rate, within fixed margins, by buying and selling gold and dollar bills. Fixed exchange rates and low tariffs were expected to favour the resurgence of free international trade.

With the exception of Latin America, the countries of the Third World did not participate in the framing of this international economic order since they had not yet gained political independence at the time. Besides, this order does not function any longer today, as is demonstrated by the escalating protectionism in the industrial countries and fluctuations in the exchange rate. After several years of supportive action in favour of the dollar on the part of other Western countries, the Nixon administration saw itself compelled, in 1971, to remove the gold exchangeability for the dollar. The system of fixed exchange rates collapsed. Likewise, tariff reduction was not effected to the full, while the economic recession has been, since the seventies fuelling protectionist tendencies in the West.

Hence today, discussions on a new order for the global economy are underway even in the West. Unlike the situation in 1944–47, the South also wants to have a say in evolving this new order today.

ORGANISATIONS FOR THE PROTECTION OF ECONOMIC INTERESTS IN THE SOUTH

The non-aligned movement and the so-called Group of 77 provided the basis for the prevailing system of alliances amongst the Third World countries of today. Both movements are now closely inter-linked with each other, the non-aligned states having assumed, since the seventies, the role of the avant garde within the Group of 77 since the seventies.

The non-aligned movement emerged at the close of the forties with a series of conferences of Asiatic countries, culminating in the first conference in Bandung (1955) of all Asian and African countries which had attained independence by then. Their subjects of deliberation were predominantly political in nature: The struggle against colonialism and racism, the defence of national sovereignty, the principles governing the conduct of new states in their inter-action with each other. Asia and Africa were to be kept out of the Cold War in the North. Nevertheless, significant economic demands had already been raised: the 'diversification of exports through raw material processing, the stabilisation of commodity prices, cooperation between the Afro-Asian countries in the form of joint industrial ventures, enhancement of credit facilities by the West, exchange of information on the petroleum industry.'

The Bandung Conference was followed by a series of Afro-Asian Solidarity Conferences which drew participation from an increasing number of states after initial difficulties. One of the reasons for this increased participation was the system of regional representation in practice in the UN: Since the General Assembly is not divided up into official factions, the non-permanent members to the Security Council and the members to the important Committees are elected on the basis of the principle of regional representation. In order to have a say in these decisions, a country has to be a member of its regional group. The Afro-Asian States, constituting one such regional group, therefore, coordinated with each other in the UN.

Nevertheless, opinion in the Third World remained divided over the issue of political relations with the West. This was amply demonstrated at the First Conference of the Heads of State of the Non-Aligned (Belgrade 1961). Only twenty-five of the forty-four independent countries of Asia and Africa participated. Several Black African countries and almost all the Latin American countries were conspicuous by their absence.

At the same time, the end of the colonial age brought a majority of the South into the UN General Assembly. The new members were strongly influenced by their colonial past. This new majority took up the demand made by the Belgrade Conference on the problems faced by the South and, in 1962, pushed through the resolution to hold a conference on trade, development and aid under the auspices of the UN. While preparing for this conference, the President of the UN Economic Commission for Latin America (CEPAL, ECLA), Raul Prebisch, drawing on the experiences of this commission, came to exert a vital influence on the framing of Third World demands, which were laid down at a preliminary conference. The seventy-seven states of the South which endorsed this document have since formed the Group of 77 which, today, consists of over a hundred and twenty members, almost all of these being the countries of the South (with the exception of Yugoslavia, which is a founder member, and the East Bloc country of Rumania).

The Conference of 1964 was institutionalised (UNCTAD) and is considered a specialised agency of the UN today. The North–South dialogue is carried on within its framework. Since 1964, six more conferences have been held at regular intervals (the last one in 1987). Besides, the UNIDO (1967) and the UNDP (1965) were set up, within the system of the UN, to serve as instruments of industrialisation in the Third World.

After the disappointing results of the First UN Decade for Development proclaimed in 1961, and the failure of the 'Alliance for Progress' (1961 USA–Latin America), the Group of 77 intensified its drive towards conference diplomacy, organised itself in all the specialised agencies of the UN, and since the beginning of the seventies, has taken to synthesizing parallel talks held in different fora into global negotiations. Around the same time, the increasing leverage of the non-aligned countries within the Group of 77 led to the politicisation of demands. Accordingly, since the seventies, the Group of 77 has succeeded in making North–South economic relations an issue of 'high politics' as well as one of the most important subjects of world politics itself.

The oil price crisis of 1973 gave the countries of the South added weight. The OPEC emerged in 1960 out of the contacts (established since 1949) between the 'old' oil-producer of the Third World, Venezuela, and the newer oil-exporting Arab countries, whose oil exports intensified after 1945. The cause for this lay in the unilateral reduction effected in the 'list price' of crude by the oil companies, the profits of the production companies being calculated on the basis of these prices, with the tax revenues of the producer countries, consequently, also depending on this factor. However, due to a surplus of cheap oil in the world market, the OPEC knew only partial success in its efforts against the oil companies during the sixties.

From the mid-sixties onwards, the growing political instability in the Near East prompted the oil companies to seek a diversification of their raw material base. Due to the high costs of other sources of energy, these companies were interested in increasing oil prices. The vital role played by them in 1969 in retaining the quota system for oil imports into the USA—to the detriment of the rest of the American industry which wanted to step up imports of cheap oil from the Middle East to reduce its high energy costs as compared to those of Japan and Western Europe—proved that even the American government was interested in a policy of relocation of a part of the oil production to the politically more stable regions of the North (Alaska, North Sea oil, oil shales, oil sands).

The first set of conferences held in 1971, in which the American government compelled the West Europeans to accept higher prices, was an indicator for the oil-producing countries that the West was willing to make concessions. Since low oil prices and good relations with the West—due to the latter's pro-Israeli stance—threatened the very stability of pro-Western Arab regimes, oil price rises were not to be made to appear as the successful effort of anti-Western forces. 'Radical' countries like Algeria, Libya and Iraq stood alongside pro-West regimes such as Imperial Iran, Saudi Arabia, and Kuwait, as the spokesmen of OPEC.

The cutback in oil production, following the outbreak of the Arab–Israeli War in October 1973, sparked off a fourfold increase in the price of oil within a period of less than three months, and resulted in a still further increase in the revenue per barrel of crude secured by the governments. It was impossible to even stabilise oil prices, leave alone increasing them in the long term, a contention which had been advanced time and again, by the West and was now proved to be mere rhetoric. Similar assertions with regard to other raw materials met a similar fate. However, the West's attempt to play off the oil-importing developing countries of the South (which were at that time burdened by high energy costs) against the rich OPEC countries came to naught. The South, as a whole, saw the oil price rise as an important step towards realising the demands they had posed to the West.

The oil-producing countries have skilfully made use of this feeling of solidarity binding the South. To be sure, the high share of development aid extended by them, measured in terms of their GNP, smacks of propaganda: Payments, in this case, are made from a land rent which is acquired through the employment of non-indigenous factors of production. On the other hand, however, this aid served as an important tool for strengthening unity within the South, as was demonstrated by the severing of diplomatic relations with Israel by all the Black African countries after 1973. Particularly under the leadership of the Algerian President Boumediene, the OPEC succeeded in bringing about a significant change in the relationship of the entire South to the West in that it forced the industrial countries of the West to enter into serious negotiations.

Following the Fourth Conference of the Non-Aligned Heads of State convened in Algiers just before the oil crisis (September 1973), the demands of the Group of 77 were carried over to the UN General Assembly. The Sixth Extraordinary Session of the General Assembly passed a resolution on the 1st of May 1974—the choice of the date was to symbolise the parallelism between the

South's struggle and the struggle of the labour movement in the North—adopting a 'Declaration on the Establishment of a New International Economic Order' and an 'Action Programme for the Establishment of a New International Economic Order'. The thirtieth meeting of the General Assembly which followed, adopted a 'Charter of the Economic Rights and Duties of States', and the seventh Extraordinary Session of the General Assembly subsequent to this (1975), passed a resolution on 'Development and International Cooperation'.

From then onwards, the industrial countries of the West started paying serious attention to the demands of the South. Fora such as the UNCTAD or the UN General Assembly, in which the industrial countries were vastly outnumbered, were no longer considered by both sides to be suitable platforms, as soon as it became clear that genuine concessions were to be negotiated. A Conference on International Economic Cooperation was convened in Paris at the initiative of France and Algeria in which nineteen developing countries (both producers and non-producers of oil) participated alongside all the industrial countries. When it became clear after two years of conference negotiation that the industrial countries, particularly under the influence of the United States and the Federal Republic of Germany, only wanted to discuss the energy issue, and were less willing to consider the entire catalogue of demands made by the Group of 77, this conference was suspended. The South returned to the forum of the UN and its specialised agencies with its demands.

THE SOUTH'S CATALOGUE OF DEMANDS

The West has been presented with a wide-ranging list of demands in several declarations drawn up by the South (the Group of 77, the majorities in the UNCTAD and other UN organisations, the majorities in the UN General Assembly). The nature of this catalogue of demands is moulded by the regional organisation of the decision-making process within the Group of 77, whereby countries with diverse development strategies and interests have to reach a compromise at an early stage. It is obvious that the social structures of the developing countries do not form the subject of deliberation at such conferences since each government considers itself to be solely responsible for this area, with respect to its country. Only the problems of the developing countries with the West (and, to a lesser extent, with the East) are accommodated in the basket of demands.

The following constitute the most important demands made by the South: Increase in the volume of development aid; debt restructuring; higher share in world industrial production and greater access to the markets of the industrial countries; control over the MNCs, especially over their monopolistic practices in technology transfer; better commodity prices; greater international liquidity through access to the IMF's special drawing rights; a stronger representation of the countries of the South in international organisations.

Since the First Decade for Development, the industrial countries of the West have sanctioned the increase of *development assistance* to 1 per cent of the GNP. None of the larger industrial countries of the West has to date achieved this objective; similarly, the objective of extending public aid to the tune of 0.7 per cent of the GNP, which was adopted in 1975 and reiterated in 1983, remained unfulfilled (1985/86; average of 0.35 per cent, USA 0. 23 per cent, FRG 0.44 per cent, Norway 1. 1 per cent). Owing to the economic recession, development assistance is increasingly being linked (though, of course, not openly) to the securing of orders for the donor's own industry, whereby the recipient is generally forced to pay higher prices for imports financed through aid.

New developments occur due to the dramatic decline of the poor countries during the 1980s. Under the leadership of the World Bank, structural adjustment programmes are initiated. Programme lending and aid have increasingly displaced more project aid. Bilateral agencies in the West are required by their governments to follow the World Bank strategy which is supported by concessional lending from the IMF. In the poor countries (especially in subsaharan Africa, but also in some Asian countries such as Bangladesh) which depend on aid sometimes to more than 10 per cent of the GNP, there has been a virtual takeover of economic policy decision-making by a more and more coordinated donor community, in which the World Bank—by virtue of its financial means and its capacity to develop macroeconomic policies—tends to be the accepted leader.

In the case of *debts*, the South demanded fresh negotiations in 1974, and the conversion of all debts into official development assistance in 1975. The industrial countries made it a rule at the outset that each individual case would be considered separately. Some of the poorest countries had their debts cancelled by some industrial countries. The South failed in its attempt to lay down general rules for debt restructuring, which would have made it impossible for international institutions to impose conditions. Recent examples from Brazil and Mexico demonstrate that, contrary to their assurances at the UNCTAD VI (1983), the industrial countries of the West do not link debt restructuring with the grant of loans for the economic revival of the South. Instead, they, on the other hand, enforce the traditional policy of devaluation and the curtailment of public spending in the debtor countries. This policy is rendered possible if only for the reason that less indebted developing countries, in turn, fear that upon the acceptance of the principle of cancellation of debts, they, too, might have to forego credit from Western banks in the future.

In the area of *industrial production*, the South demanded an increase in its share from 7 per cent at the time (1975) to 25 per cent. This necessitated an increase in the annual growth rates of industrial production, far higher than the 8 per cent strived for in the Second UN Decade for Development. In Asia (including the Middle East) an annual rate of 6 per cent was achieved between 1975–1982, for the Third World as a whole this figure was 5. 5 per cent , p. a., with growth rates declining since 1978. It was only for the period 1975–1978, and that too, only in the case of Asia, that growth rates, at 10. 5 per cent, p. a., were higher than 8 per cent. Growth rates in the 1980s were rather low, 1. 6 per cent per annum for industrial production (Third World average) and 5. 1 per cent for manufacturing. But regional differences were considerable, with manufacturing stagnating (Latin America 1. 1 per cent, p. a.), or in decline (subsaharan Africa), whereas in Asia manufacturing grew at 10. 1 per cent p. a., due to the even higher growth rates in the four leading export-oriented countries of Southeast and East Asia. The developing countries demanded a conscious policy of relocation of labour-intensive and raw material-intensive production lines (and even the processing of indigenous raw materials). This goal was achieved to the extent that it was in line with export-oriented industrialisation.

Indeed, as demanded by the South, the industrial countries of the West did extend unilateral generalised preferences to the developing countries to promote the export of manufactures. However, these regulations are rendered ineffective in the case of those very products which are of interest to the developing countries, by the quantitative restrictions imposed by the industrial countries. It is the abolition of these restrictions which the South has expressly demanded. The processing of raw materials in the producer countries continues to be hampered by duties on manufactured products. Even fat imported in small packs, or decaffeinated coffee beans, leave alone roasted coffee, are levied duties of 10–20 per cent as a result of which the actual process of manufacturing itself receives almost double the tariff protection (the value of the finished product also includes the price of the raw material, which is also subject to taxation when a manufactured product is imported).

There has also been no conscious relocation of industries which could have linkage effects in the developing countries. Manufactured exports from the developing countries rose as a proportion of the GNP of the industrial countries from 0. 7 per cent in 1975 to 1. 25 per cent in 1980, with the FRG leading here with 1.6 per cent. However, under the impact of the recession, this percentage dropped in 1981 for all the industrial countries of the West (average: 0.8 per cent). It reached 0. 95 per cent in 1985 for all OECD countries, with the United States leading (1.6 per cent), the European Community being at an intermediate position (0.7 per cent), with varying levels (Germany, 0.8 per cent, France, 0.4 per cent), and Japan being rather closed (0.4 per cent). The share of the Third World manufacturing exports in apparent consumption of manufactures rose from 2.36 per cent in 1980/81, 2.39 per cent in 1982/83, to 2.93 per cent in 1984/85. Here also, the United States lead (2.31 per cent, 2.49 per cent, 3.38 per cent), the European Community (2.74 per cent, 2.73 per cent, 3.04 per cent) and Japan (1.69 per cent, 1.59 per cent, 1.63 per cent). These values show rising protectionism in the European Community, high protectionism in Japan, and U.S. preparedness to engage in a new international division of labour. This preparedness has, however, been on the decline in the last year.

In an effort to *exercise control over the MNCs*, the South strove for an international agreement on the rules of conduct for foreign investors, the so-called 'Code of Conduct'. The industrial countries cited problems of a legal nature which, they claimed, made it impossible for them to interfere directly in the business policies of private companies, thus emptying the draft of all substance. The proposed regulations would, in effect, have served to fight the misuse of market power, the prevention of which is as much the responsibility of state authorities in the West as of those in the South. The West watered down all acts of malpractice, for instance by replacing 'the impairment of innovation' with the 'unreasonable impairment of innovation', with reference to technology purchased by an underdeveloped country. In the event of obvious cases of malpractice, possibilities of intervention open to the governments of the South were to be linked with the imposition of additional conditions.

The developing countries adopted a very cautious stance where the *improvement of commodity prices* was concerned. Apart from improved marketing opportunities and the intensification of research on additional avenues for raw material utilisation, as against the utilisation of synthetics, these countries demanded 'stable, remunerative and fair prices'. The formation of cartels for the appropriation of rent was never officially an issue of debate, even though the right to form producer associations had been incorporated into the Charter of the Rights and Duties of States. Several modes of indexation were discussed, as for instance, the linking up of commodity prices with the prices of imported goods, and of the prices of finished products manufactured from raw materials, with production costs, or changes in the exchange rates.

Export quotas, uniform export duties of the raw material-producing countries, international marketing agencies and buffer stockpiles were suggested as possible measures of enforcement. The South reached an agreement on the demand for a 'Common Fund'. Buffer stocks were to be set up for a number of important raw materials to effect price stability. Since the financing of these buffer stock arrangements appeared to be expensive, a Common Fund was to be created for this purpose. Depending on the market conditions, and given different price movements for different commodities, revenue from the sale of well-priced commodities could be utilised for purchasing low-priced commodities.

This show of restraint on the part of the South, where commodity prices are concerned, can be explained by three factors. Firstly, in its Commercial Law of 1974, the USA excluded from its system of generalised preferences all those countries belonging to producer unions which inflated prices to 'unreasonable' levels. If a country wished to diversify its economy through manufactured exports, then it was required to refrain from participating in commodity cartels. Wide sections of the scientific world in the Western industrial countries participated in a world-wide campaign on the subject of crude oil constituting a special commodity. Under the influence of Saudi Arabia, the oil-producing countries refused to lend their combined support, arguing that higher prices for other raw materials would erode the purchasing power in the industrial countries of the West, thereby narrowing down the marketing avenues for oil.

On the other hand, the oil-producing countries could very well have financed a coffee cartel. Before 1975, revenue from coffee export amounted to $ 8 billion. Coffee can be stored for a period of two years. A fourfold increase in the world market price of raw coffee in 1974–78 was borne by the consumers. Financing a coffee cartel in the event of a possible boycott in the industrial countries would have only cost the oil-producing countries a fraction of the amount invested every year in the banks and public debts of the industrial countries. The absence of empirical studies on the possibilities of price increase for instance, only demonstrates the cautious stance of the UNCTAD in the commodity issue. Nevertheless, attempts have been made—partly in collaboration with the industrial countries—to appropriate rents in commodity export (as in the case of iron, quicksilver, wood among others). Bauxite presented the most interesting case. Caribbean producers succeeded in increasing governmental revenue from the export of bauxite, as can be anticipated in accordance with the Theory of Differential Rent. However, the union collapsed because an African 'socialist' country, Guinea, did not adhere to the production schedule.

Despite the restricted nature of demands in the commodity sector, the agreement on the establishment of a Common Fund was reached only in 1980. The agreement stipulated that the Western industrial countries would bear 68 per cent of the financial costs, in return for which they would be entitled to a majority veto, with 42 per cent of the voting power (all important decisions require a two-third, or a three-fourth majority). By 1983, one hundred and eight countries had signed the agreement, however, with only five ratifying it, so much so that its implementation with effect from 1 July 1984 remained an uncertainty, even at that time. In the last years, no more consideration was given to the project.

The industrial countries did give consideration to the demand for an increase in international liquidity through an *enhanced level of credit from the IMF* (additional special drawing rights), immediately following the oil price rises of 1973 (the various oil facilities of the IMF). The motive underlying this was to finance the balance of trade deficits with which not only the oil-importing countries, but even the West (Italy, for example), were unable to cope, in the short term. However, a long-term increase in international liquidity was thwarted by the USA, which feared that an expansion in the volume of IMF funds would only exacerbate inflationary tendencies worldwide, although emergency lending for debt-ridden countries and structural adjustment did take place.

With regard to the *restructuring of the system of the UN*, the South was, on the one hand, interested in an increase in the financial resources of institutions like the UNDP and the UNIDO in which the Group of 77 enjoyed majorities, and, on the other, in greater leverage in funding institutions such as the World Bank and the IMF. The South was successful only in the latter case, for the *IMF quotas* have been fixed in proportion to the financial strength of the member countries: In 1976, the main oil-exporting countries were expressly granted higher quotas, for which they were also required to pay higher subscriptions. This, however, could not jeopardise the 50 per cent majority of the main contributors (USA 19. 9 per cent, Great Britain 6. 9 per cent, FRG 6. 0 per cent, France 5. 0 per cent, Canada 3. 3 per cent, Japan 4. 7 per cent), a percentage requisite for carrying decisions.

The South's offensive, launched at the beginning of the seventies, failed because the countries of the Third World were riven by divergent interests, many of them even more interested in North–South economic cooperation than the West. As a result, important developing countries, particularly the financially powerful Arab States of the Gulf, were won over for a policy of moderation.

Some industrial countries of the West were more inclined to accept the demands of the Third World (the Scandinavian countries, the Netherlands). After the oil price rise of 1973, France, Italy and Spain were willing to enter into extensive bilateral cooperation with the developing countries at the governmental level. France and Italy, for instance, were ready to accept higher commodity prices (rather than having the markets of the industrial countries opened to manufactured exports from the Third World), if the additional revenue accruing from this source was used for purchasing the products of their capital goods industry, which was weaker in both these countries. Such agreements have been concluded time and again, in the case of France this also extended to agreements on arms export. The Franco–Algerian and the Algerian–Italian natural gas agreements are a case in point. Meanwhile, differences between France, on the one hand, and the FRG and the USA, on the other, have subsided. The leading producers of capital goods have increased their exports into the rich oil countries, in many cases, without concluding wide-ranging agreements. Since these oil countries always wanted to buy the most modern technology at the most favourable terms, it was France and Italy which were at a disadvantage and increasingly dependent on solidarity within the Western camp.

THE NEW INTERNATIONAL ECONOMIC ORDER: A FAILURE?

The industrial countries of the West had sufficient grounds to oppose what had grown to be an unrestrainable and uncontrollable transfer of funds from the West to the South. The growth in the access of the Third World 'State–classes' to finance does not necessarily lead to economic development. Even high oil revenues could only partially induce productive investment. In the case of some countries, for example, Algeria, these high revenues only succeeded in making the tendency towards inefficiency more pronounced.

There are three causes for the West's interest in the NIEO which, in accordance with the aspirations of the South, must be realised within the framework of global talks. To achieve this end, the South, on its part, must also be willing to negotiate on the employment of additional resources. With a debt service of $ 172 billion in 1988, debts can be repaid neither through a massive increase in manufactured exports nor in commodity exports.

Today, these debts are causing a decline in the imports of the main debtor countries from the industrial countries of the West. This serves to strengthen recessionary tendencies even in the West, as a result of which there is a fall in the exports of developing countries. The readiness with which the developing countries entered into debt in the seventies muted the recessionary trends which had set in in the industrial countries. Debt collection strengthens these recessionary tendencies and has only limited success. If the banks wish to recover their money (in the case of some large banks, making up 10 per cent of borrowings) through the increase in the export revenues of the non-oil exporters of the South, then the prices of raw materials other than crude oil must rise.

As was evidenced in 1973, between the oil companies and the oil-producing countries, important 'capital groups' in the industrial countries and the raw material-producing countries could come to a tacit understanding, or even take to parallel action, thereby facilitating the transfer of resources to the countries of the South at the expense of the Western consumer. A transfer of resources through newly created raw material cartels would, however, lead to problems similar to those confronting the OPEC countries, without effecting any fundamental changes: The politicisation of economic relations and the lack of adequate resources utilisation for overcoming underdevelopment.

Possibilities of raising commodity prices do actually exist. Where high price rises are possible, political discord between the principal exporters is overcome. The possibility of a price increase of even just 300 per cent, as in the case of coffee in 1975–1978, would certainly enable a country with a small market share to effect a greater increase in revenue, in the short term, by selling below the cartel price than by observing the disciplinary measures laid down by the cartels. Success gained in this manner would, however, be very short-lived. The fact that a producer cartel can survive even strife between its members, given a sufficiently high rate of return, has been demonstrated by the OPEC whose 1981 cutback in prices was not primarily due to differences amongst its members, but was to serve the objective of slackening the efforts of the industrial countries to develop alternative sources of energy.

Today, the industrial countries of the West are themselves interested in seeing mass poverty eradicated in the Third World. Hitherto, the growth mechanism of the West's industrial countries (rise in mass incomes on par with the rise in labour productivity, ± changes in capital productivity and terms of trade, or reduction in the number of working hours) could be sustained because all industrial countries had similar social structures and real incomes rose in all competing nations. But no sooner does the transfer of technology to the South become possible than — given rising mass incomes or lesser number of working hours in the West and stagnating labour incomes (and longer hours of work) in the South—the difference in labour costs between the West and the production sites of the South (1/16 to 1/57 as compared to the USA at the end of the 1970s) grows larger than the difference in productivity (which is often lower).

If the trade unions of the West were to effect an increase in wages, or a reduction in the hours of work on par with the rise in productivity, with the aim of ensuring an adequate level of total demand, they would only be hastening the process of relocation. Alternatively, if they were to exercise restraint in wage negotiations, they would be contributing to an underconsumptionist crisis in the industrial countries. The labour movement in the West cannot, by itself, fight the demand gap which is clearly emerging at the global level today. However, in the South, the effects of the relocation of production sites from the West are too small to effect a lasting change in the structure of the labour markets. Consequently, the workers of the South are also not in a position to solve the problem posed by the gap between the productive and consumptive capacities of the economies of the West and the South, which are more closely linked to each other through export-oriented industrialisation. As a result of mass poverty and the insignificant effect of relocation in relation to unemployment in the South, *the gap between productive capacity and consumptive capacity has been growing worldwide.*

The argument that mass incomes in the West are being eroded by the relocation of manufacturing production without a corresponding growth in the purchasing power of the Third World, has been rebutted. In this connection, it has been stressed that the volume of manufactured exports from the Third World to the industrial countries is still, on the whole, insignificant. By playing down the effects of a development strategy whose range is still small, one cannot dismiss the dangers which are likely to emanate from such a strategy. Furthermore, it is contended that developing countries exporting finished products import goods whose volume corresponds with that of the exports. This argument overlooks the fact that products are rendered cheaper by the relocation of production sites. The revenue earned by the developing countries from manufactured exports is lower than the income previously paid in this production sector in the industrial countries.

The balance of trade deficit of the developing countries forms the basis of the contention that these countries import a greater quantity of manufactured exports from the industrialised Western countries than they export to them. These statistics also include the OPEC countries; they explain the necessity of market expansion through commodity price increases. Besides, these figures also cover the highly indebted newly industrialising countries: Does the maintenance of an adequate level of world demand hinge on further financial flows from the industrial countries? However, neither of these arguments refutes the fact that with persisting mass poverty and unemployment in the developing countries, export-oriented industrialisation will accelerate recessionary tendencies in the world economy.

Competition between production sites in the newly industrialising countries and the industrial countries of the West cannot, in the long run, be stifled by protectionist measures: The leading industrial countries can aim at 'structural change' on the basis of their technological advantage. In the process, they also draw support from the markets of the weaker industrial countries. The latter are, in turn, prevented from effecting such a structural change. Wedged between the hammer of the high-tech production of the leading industrial nations and the anvil of the low-cost production of traditional industrial products in the developing countries, these weaker industrial economies find their industrial growth opportunities to be drastically reduced. It is here that the process of 'downward equalisation' sets in, as borne out by the relocation of textile and shoe production to low-cost and low-income family enterprises in Italy (a recent trend of 'putting-out production').

In their struggle for the control of markets for new products which are not expected to afford competitive advantages to the Third World in the near future, all industrial countries set store by low production costs, i.e., by wage cuts. The race for devaluation in the thirties has been replaced by the race for cost curtailment, at the expense of mass incomes in the industrial countries of the West. This only has the effect of aggravating the current world economic recession. Further, the impact of this race on employment in the industrial countries is, at present, of greater importance than that of Third World manufactured exports, though it is triggered off by the latter.

The introduction of micro-processors will hardly increase the competitiveness of production sites in the West: Higher productivity necessitates even higher increases in real incomes in the West, while micro-processors release skilled labour whose scarcity in the South has until now restricted the process of relocation.

THE NEW INTERNATIONAL ECONOMIC ORDER AND THE ERADICATION OF MASS POVERTY IN THE THIRD WORLD

The West cannot, on its own, ward off the threat of a shortage in world demand and prevent the transfer of large amounts of resources to the South in the long run. It should, therefore, make concessions in various areas contingent on the willingness of the South to increase the level of employment and incomes of the general masses. Development strategies suited to this end should be oriented towards the reproduction of the link between growth and technological development in the South through mass production for mass consumption.

The inflexibility of economies in the South does not allow for mass incomes to be increased merely through a redistribution of income. The case of Chile under Allende proves that without a planned restructuring of the productive apparatuses to meet mass demand, which may then only emerge on the market as the outcome of political and economic strategies, a redistribution of income will only lead to inflation and/or a burgeoning balance of trade deficit. A planned restructuring of the productive apparatuses calls for investment, which can be financed through development aid, loans and debt restructuring, technology transfer on concessional terms, higher commodity prices and increased exports. A strategy of this type, however, also requires the political will of the governments of the South to invest such resources in the expansion of mass employment and in the development of appropriate productive apparatuses.

An increase in the production and the incomes of the rural population constitute the very crux of a strategy which aims at overcoming underdevelopment. In many Third World countries, this necessitates land reform, or the abolition of state marketing agencies which keep the prices of agricultural products artificially depressed. The mass of the poor lives in the rural areas. A high proportion of additional mass income (60–90 per cent) goes towards the purchase of foodstuffs. Agriculture is the key sector, both from the perspective of production for mass consumption, as well as from the perspective of the creation of mass incomes.

The economic objective of *a policy of land reform and improved agricultural prices* lies in motivating the farmers to put in more work on their land, even as a form of investment (to fight land erosion, to secure irrigation facilities). Several studies have testified that Third World farmers respond to price incentives and intensify land utilisation if they stand to gain by the additional output. Everywhere in the Third World, farm yields are the highest in small-scale units, even though the overall average is low. In most cases, a long-term increase in agricultural output however requires additional industrial inputs such as fertilisers, irrigation pipes, pumps and tractors; only when these are produced indigenously will the balance of payment position remain favourable, despite a rapid modernisation of agriculture. Where the toolmaking industry is concerned, either indigenous or adapted technology can be employed. Apart from developing a sector producing agricultural inputs, production capacities for mass-consumption goods must also be set up since the farmers will not be willing to invest more work in return for mere paper money.

A portion of the industrial capital and consumer goods can be produced in *the urban and rural small-scale sector* in which more employment will be generated due to higher mass demand. This sector can be made more dynamic if new intermediate inputs and capital goods from local production are made available. Hence, the modern sector of industry should be oriented to the production of such partially 'adapted' products.

Even the *modern sector* would have better growth opportunities with an increase in mass incomes and a restriction of luxury consumption than it does at present, with the markedly inequitable income distribution. In the event of a redistribution of consumer demand, there emerges a demand for a small range of products in keeping with the initially low level of mass income, these products, however, being elicited only in large batches. Here, the advantages of large-batch production, particularly where expensive capital goods are employed, could be capitalised on. Due to the concentration of the demand on a narrow spectrum of products, industrial development can be restricted, initially, to a small number of production lines. In this case, the demand for (scarce) skilled labour is lower than what it would be in the case of a strongly diversified demand created by the high incomes of the top income groups.

Since the demand for consumer goods is more homogenous in the case of an egalitarian income distribution, the demand for intermediate inputs and capital goods will likewise also be more homogenous. This facilitates the local production of such goods, based on the larger production series. Due to the lower quality demands of the poor as regards manufactured products, simple technologies can be used. Therefore, even in the face of the prevailing low level of technological development, an expansion of mass demand enables the local production of capital goods and intermediate inputs. This, in turn, results in learning effects in production for a relatively large number of workers. Skills acquired in this manner can serve as basis for a process of ongoing upgradation of technical skills which encompasses the import of foreign technology, its reproduction and adaptation to local conditions.

An 'egalitarist' development strategy does not presuppose a total disassociation from the West but, rather, a controlled form of cooperation. Instead of a country merely confining itself to the 'consumption' of imported technologies, the 'assimilation' of technology should also be made possible by building up local capacities for capital goods and intermediate inputs. The assimilation of technology refers to the capacity of local industries to repair imported capital goods, adapt them to local conditions and develop them further. Learning effects could, especially, be great in the case of a slightly outdated technology.

On the basis of an analysis of the demand profiles and product paths, one can determine the branches of production which are to be developed to satisfy a mass demand that emerges as the outcome of social reform. The composition and level of demand created in the event of a rise in mass incomes can be roughly estimated on the basis of a study of demand from households whose income today is as high as projected mass incomes in the wake of reforms. The product path describes the course of the raw material passing through different stages of processing during which various technologies are employed and various intermediate goods utilised. If the composition and level of projected mass demand is known, then the demand for capital goods and intermediate inputs can be determined by following the product path from the opposite direction. In this manner, goods which can only be produced with modern technology can be identified as against those which can be produced with modern and traditional, and, perhaps, even adapted technologies.

The modern industrial sector should, accordingly, be primarily oriented to products which are amongst those necessary for satisfying a rising mass demand and which can only be produced with modern technology. For most countries, the foreign exchange position determines the extent to which modern technology is to be employed to boost economic growth, even in those sectors in which production is possible with local technology. However, the oil-producing countries furnish proof of the fact that even with extremely large foreign exchange reserves, the mere import of technology without the back-up of an indigenous capital goods production will only result in the non-assimilation of imported technology not being assimilated due to the absence of a broad-based class of skilled labour.

An analysis of the product path of goods required in case of rising mass demand provides the basis for the definition of 'egalitarist' production chains, i.e., production chains whose existence is necessary to meet a rising mass demand. Such egalitarist production chains can even include industrial plants, such as steel works and cement factories, which have been erected for other purposes.

Employment is generated by a strategy of overcoming underdevelopment through mass consumption, by the development of local technology for the small-scale sector, by the orientation of large-scale enterprises to mass consumption, and by the demand of a reformed agricultural sector and a progressively modern small-scale sector for capital goods and intermediate inputs. Such a strategy enables the mass of the population to produce for its own needs utilising partly outdated technologies. Full employment, without an increased dependence on capital goods imports, can be attained through agrarian reform and greater labour input in agriculture, through a modernising small-scale sector and local technology production. An expansion in the exports of labour-intensive products goods would, then, expose the country concerned to a labour market where, as a result of the scarcity of labour, and with rising demand even for unskilled workers, there is an increase in the latter's wages. A growth in exports leads to rising real incomes and the expansion of domestic markets. Investments made to meet this additional demand, in turn, create jobs. The tendency towards a strengthening of growth impulses from additional export demand, so characteristic of the developed economies, would then emerge in the developing countries as well.

Export-oriented industrialisation could play a role in overcoming underdevelopment if rising mass demand in the Third World provides a solution for the employment problem. Export-oriented industrialisation, in this case, would not jeopardise the maintenance of a liberal world economy, for the growth in exports in the South would lead to a corresponding growth in real incomes there.

As an outcome of the mere transfer of resources from the West to the South, structural reforms requisite for such development strategies could be dispensed with because it is possible to pursue the strategy of industrialisation hitherto in force. It is, therefore, crucial for the relationship between the West and the developing world to determine whether the demands put forth by the South to the West can be successfully linked to social structural change in the South, in such a manner that the problem of poverty can be solved through rising mass incomes and an appropriate restructuring of the productive apparatuses.

The conflict between 'the West' and 'the developing countries' should give way to a merger between the forces in the West and the South which would collectively strive for full employment and rising mass consumption all over the world. With their combined effort these forces should then successfully implement such a solution for overcoming the prevailing world economic recession and under-development in the South.

5

Towards a Reform Strategy for the West

Which forces can be mobilised in the West and in the South? How can these be mobilised in such a manner as to link up the transfer of financial resources to the governments of the South with social structural reforms in the underdeveloped countries? These are some of the questions that arise out of the discussion in the preceding pages, and it is to these that we now turn.

STATE–CLASS Vs. LOWER CLASS: REPRESSION AND REFORM IN THE THIRD WORLD

In today's Third World there are State–classes which, due to the control they exercise over the economy and the clientelist ties binding them to all other groups, prevent the lower classes from organising protest movements. Protest is often met with repression from these State–classes, rather than with reforms, for these classes are primarily interested in preserving their power. To give in to open protest would, effectively, be signalling to all the other social groups that the State–class is no longer capable of holding on to its power, thereby giving rise to the fear that this might trigger off a chain reaction of protest.

If peaceful forms of protest such as strikes, production boy-cotts and demonstrations prove ineffective in extracting reforms from State–classes, some people may be led to assume that social change lies in the armed struggle of the rural population and the 'marginalised', i.e., the urban unemployed, and those engaged in the informal sector.

The guerilla war, an example of such armed protest, is looked upon as a special mode of resistance offered by the 'damned of this world' (Fanon). However, to date, guerilla warfare has never succeeded against the State–classes in bureaucratic development societies. The effectiveness of guerilla warfare has often been overestimated in Western social sciences, for their basis of measurement has been decolonisation and the success of the Chinese Revolution. Guerilla wars waged against the colonial powers served to increase the costs of the colonial system. Constituting a form of warfare in which (often) 'deracinated' intellectuals organise the rural poor and middle farmers into small combat groups, which can often jeopardise local public security. This puts them in a position where they can either employ intimidatory tactics to keep local functionaries of the existing system from continuing to work for the powers that be, or liquidate them physically.

The ruling government is isolated. It is 'blinded' because it does not know who among the local population supports the guerillas. The revolutionary core of the guerilla organise the rest of the local population and sets up its own administrative and legal system, while erecting a wall of silence around the area, in order to cut off the government in the city. History demonstrates that the guerillas have only been successful where, aside from material interests, other motivating factors have also had a hand in determining the degree of involvement of the population, or where the governments in power only had limited means of repression at hand.

Viewed from the perspective of the restriction of means, Third World State–classes distinguish themselves from colonial administrations and 'oligarchies' in the following manner. It is true that the colonial administration was backed by powerful industrial countries. However, these countries were not sufficiently interested in preserving colonial rule so as to deploy their entire potential forces to quell protest in their colonial territories. Only in two instances—the Algerian War (1954–62) and the Vietnam War (1965–73)—were the industrial countries of the West willing to despatch their conscript armies into a Third World war zone for a long period. In the case of Third World State–classes, on the other hand, their very survival depends on suppressing the guerillas. Accordingly, the entire military potential at their disposal is deployed.

The 'wall of silence' within which the guerillas imprison the local population is impenetrable only to a certain extent. The colonial administration have demonstrated, in individual cases, how this 'wall' may be penetrated: namely, through torture and acts of retaliation. In both cases, a colonial administration, or an intervening Western power, as the case may be, invites sharp criticism from the home country. This criticism compels the colonial or the Western intervening power to exercise restraint while employing such repressive methods. It also strengthens the local population in their belief that the revolutionary guerillas will be victorious, as a result of which the local people are more willing to involve themselves in the guerilla cause.

On the other hand, the State–classes, such as the military regimes of Argentina (23,000 missing since 1976) or Brazil (1964–68), are not deterred from employing any means at their disposal to fight the guerillas. They are in a position to suppress criticism within the country and, unlike foreign powers, are not dependent on public opinion in the West. In this case, the local population quickly grasps the situation and does not expect the State–class concerned to be the ultimate loser. Oligarchies, i.e., small classes of exploiters cashing in on their land holdings and their control over a small state apparatus, which are marked by a singular lack of great ambitions on the development policy front, also do not hesitate to employ every means at their disposal. But, due to the very fact that they have not introduced even development policy measures, their repressive means are, on the whole, limited, since they are afraid of maintaining large armies of their own, and do not favour the rise of a 'new' middle class through an expanding corps of military officers. The level of military spending in the Central American Republics is clearly lower than in the Black African, Asian or South American countries all of which have high state shares of GNP.

Although the high imports of arms from the industrial countries into the Third World are primarily attributable to regional conflicts (the Near East accounting for 48 per cent of total imports in 1970–79), many Third World governments have been training an increasing proportion of their armed forces for engagement in internal wars, and have taken up the production of arms to equip themselves for such conflicts. Even outside the Near East region, defence expenditure made up 20 per cent to 30 per cent of state expenditure in Asia, whereas in the case of Africa and Latin America this figure was 10 per cent–20 per cent (1977). This level did not change during the 1980s. As a proportion of GNP, military expenditure is, however, lower in the developing countries (around 2 per cent, 1981–82) than in the industrial countries (USA 6.6 per cent, FRG 3.4 per cent, USSR 8.7 per cent), and is especially low in the most 'traditional' countries where ruling oligarchies cannot trust their armies.

Often, material interests constitute an important factor of motivation, as far as the mobilisation of the lower classes for guerilla warfare goes. However, large sections of the population would be willing to stake their lives for material gains only if chances of success are reckoned to be very bright. In the post-1945 period, this was especially true of the colonial empires regarded as obsolete or of the Kuomintang rule in China (which was attacked by severe convulsions).

Ethnic and religious ties are motivating factors that have a stronger impact than material interests. In the struggle against the colonial powers, the racial discrimination to which the colonised peoples were subjected, at the hands of the foreigners, certainly played a role. The Shah of Iran was toppled by the Shiite clergy which could have, no doubt, capitalised on the material discontent among the lower classes, though religious motives were employed as the predominant force of mobilisation. The ethnic diversity of many African countries and the Indian problem in some Central and Andean States formed the basis of organisation for armed resistance.

Ethnic ties can be used as a weapon against State–classes only in certain restricted areas. It is the West and not the State–classes which, even today, is considered the alien power. Generally in the political field, State–classes accommodate influential religions quite successfully in their nationalistic concept of development (for example, traditional elements of legitimation, 'syncretistic' rule). Besides, religiously motivated opposition does not, for the most part occur, amongst the lower classes, but rather in those sections of the 'new middle class' which have not obtained jobs commensurate with their level of training.

Armed resistance against State–classes has little chance of success, considering the high repressive potential of State–classes, the fact that systematic attempts are made to wipe out rival organisations, and the few opportunities at hand to bring factors other than material interests into play against them at the national level. Thus, those segments of State–classes which have vested interests in social structural change make critical partners for social structural reform in the Third World. This, however, does not exempt the development of the capacity of underprivileged groups/classes to articulate their interests, through project and training assistance, as well as through transnational relations between the social groups in the West and the organisations of lower classes in the South.

EAST–WEST RIVALRY IN THE SOUTH; THE ROLE OF THE STATE–CLASSES IN SOCIAL REFORM

In their relationship with the developing countries, both the camps in the North aim at preventing the ascent to power of the forces sympathetic to the opposite bloc. This often leads to a situation in which both these camps become vulnerable to considerable political blackmail at the hands of the governments of the South. The countries of the South are economically weak; yet, their diplomatic strength is considerable, and it is born out of this very weakness. Every government of the South can—in the event of its receiving a very low level of aid from its partner in the North—threaten to expand relations with the partner's adversary from the opposite camp, claiming this action to be justified by the fact that it would have been unable to even survive on the aid offered by its old partner.

Both camps could take on most Third World regimes as partners. The (Soviet) theory of the Non-Capitalist Development Path and the several Western proponents of the Theory of Modernisation either actively demand, or accept, an increase in the level of public investment, state planning, state-owned enterprises and controlled co-operation with the MNCs. Consequently, the rivalry between the two camps has given rise to an extremely complex pattern of relations.

Formerly, the Soviet Union viewed the non-communist rulers of the independent states of Asia, Africa and Latin America as mere 'lackeys' of the imperialists, this irrespective of the relationship of these rulers with the West. After the death of Stalin, the theory of the partition of the world into two camps was discarded and contact with the non-aligned countries intensified. A major breakthrough for the Soviets was the building up of close relations with Nasser's

Egypt (1955), thereafter, with Guinea (1959) and, then, with Castro's Cuban revolutionaries (1959), whose switch-over to the Soviet camp was due more to the provocation of the USA than a matter of volition. Since the mid-sixties, the Soviet Union's policy in Asia and Africa has been one of protecting the sea-route from the Black Sea to the Pacific, a policy which also aimed at the simultaneous diplomatic isolation of the People's Republic of China. Inevitably, the USSR offered assistance to all those governments or liberation movements on which the West had turned its back and, in this manner, attempted to expand its influence in these parts of the world.

The efforts of the Soviet Union to widen its zone of influence were facilitated by regional conflicts in the Third World over regional hegemony, or over border issues. The countries engaged in conflict always try to obtain the support of a world power from the North. But apart from Cuba, the Soviet Union has, up to now, not succeeded in establishing long-term binding relations with Third World regimes which were formerly non-communist. Subsequently, even Egypt, Guinea and Somalia were lost. Experience proved that Soviet aid accepted by Third World countries did not, thereafter, bring in the gains expected for Soviet foreign policy. This led the USSR to adopt a policy of restraint even with regard to the 'socialist countries' of the South (or, as recently, in the case of Mozambique).

Time and again, Soviet setbacks have been attributable to the economic preponderance of the West. True, the Soviet Union endorses the demands put forth by the South to the West. But as far as the Soviet Union is concerned, it distances itself from such demands with the argument that underdevelopment in the Third World is the result of colonialism for which the socialist countries no longer bear any responsibility, having abolished capitalism themselves. One may well deplore the exploitation of the South in terms of low commodity prices but the COMECON countries themselves do not pay prices that are any higher. Furthermore, they are willing to import only limited quantities of raw material from the Third World.

Although the *commodity imports of the COMECON countries* from the Third World rose, in the period 1970–80 (by 367 per cent, excluding fuel; by 416 per cent, including fuel), at a much higher rate than in the Western industrial countries (218 per cent and 791 per cent, respectively), with the West still providing the only large market, especially for agricultural commodities. The industrial countries of the West accounted for 73.2 per cent of the Third World's commodity exports in 1970, 60.0 per cent in 1981, and 63.4 per cent in 1987, whereas the COMECON countries accounted for 11.2 per cent in 1970, 13.5 per cent in 1981 and 9.2 per cent in 1987, (excluding fuels). Moreover, the Soviet Union is not only endowed with abundant mineral resources but also utilises its mineral wealth to earn foreign exchange on the Western markets in direct competition with the South. This is borne out by the competition between Soviet and Algerian natural gas supplies to Western Europe.

The role of the COMECON countries in the promotion of *manufactured imports from the Third World* is lesser still. The increase in imports between 1970–1981 was + 629 per cent, 1980–87, + 81.2 per cent; i.e., 8.9 per cent p.a.; for the Western industrial countries this was + 1350 per cent; 1980–87, + 136 per cent, i.e., 13.1 per cent p.a. The shares of the COMECON countries (4.8 per cent in 1970, 2.9 per cent in 1981 and 3.9 per cent in 1987) are low and show a tendency to decline.

Similarly, the COMECON countries share of *development assistance* also declined from 11.9 per cent in 1970, to 7.4 per cent in 1981, rising slightly to 9.7 per cent in 1985–86. During the 1980s, the level of total development aid from the USSR was lower than that of Austria or Switzerland. Even the best of terms for loan repayment do not offset this low level of aid which, moreover, is concentrated in a few countries and linked with the commitment to import goods from the COMECON countries.

Even as *suppliers of modern technology, the COMECON countries* play an insignificant role. Their share of the machinery and transport equipment imports of the Third World declined from 7.9 per cent in 1970, to 4.7 per cent in 1980, and 3.2 per cent in 1987, the actual proportion of capital goods alone being lower than in the case of the Western industrial countries because of the high proportion of Soviet arms exported to the Third World.

Besides, the COMECON countries also worsen the balance of trade deficits of the Third World. Their trade surplus vis-a-vis the South rose from $ 2.1 billion in 1970 to $ 6.8 billion in 1980, and $ 16.1 billion in 1987 (in 1971, the industrial countries of the West had a trade surplus of $ 2.6 billion, whereas in 1980, the balance of trade deficit of the West amounted to $ 96.6 billion, and in 1987 to

$ 18 billion). Excluding the OPEC countries their trade surplus rose from $ 0.8 billion in 1971, to $ 5.6 billion in 1980, and $ 13.5 billion in 1987 (Western industrial countries: $ 7.4 billion in 1971, $ 35.4 billion in 1980, and a deficit of $ 4 billion in 1987). In 1987, exports to the East Bloc countries covered only 56.3 per cent of the imports of the non-OPEC developing countries from the East Bloc (101.6 per cent in the case of the Western industrial countries).

While credit from the industrial countries of the West allowed for a net inflow of foreign exchange into the developing countries even as late as in 1981, the COMECON countries earned hard currency in the developing countries, and utilised this to repay their debts to the Western countries. The debt crisis has reversed the role of the Western industrial countries for the Third World, as the latter loses hard currencey for debt repayment. Although the drain of resources is most detrimental to the Third World, it is not caused by the need of the Western industrial countries to earn foreign exchange in order to pay for balance of trade deficits in other regions. In the West–South relationship over foreign exchange, there is no lack of resources, but rather a poor distribution of purchasing power on the global scale. In the case of East–South relations, the Soviet Union cannot afford to transfer resources which would later result in increasing export obligations for its economy.

Nor will the Soviet Union serve as an economic alternative to the West for the capital–seeking countries of the Third World in the future. 'Real socialism' is characterised by low capital productivity. Industrial growth is achieved by increasing even the levels of investment. The ratio of investment to production grows worse. Scarcity of capital is a perpetual problem besetting 'real socialism'. A redistribution of income on an international scale could not possibly be of interest to such societies. By contrast, capitalist systems suffer from surplus capital and surplus production. They are more willing to accept a redistribution of income on an international scale. Economic opportunities in the West can be availed to effect social reform in the Third World if the pro-reform segments of the State–classes are duly supported.

TOWARDS A REFORM-ORIENTED ALLIANCE WITH STATE–CLASSES IN THE THIRD WORLD

To contend that effecting a link between new regulations in foreign trade relations and social reforms in the South amounts to an intolerable interference in the internal affairs of the South is to overlook the fact that, in view of the significance of North–South economic relations, each and every foreign trade regulation has a bearing on the 'internal affairs' of many countries of the South. There are no instances in which the internal affairs of the South remain totally unaffected. For, the South is even influenced by the theory propounded in Western universities and research institutes which maintains that growth is primarily conditioned by investment, and that the level and structure of consumer demand is inconsequential. Development strategies aiming at the expansion of mass demand are countered with arguments from the West and considered to be not feasible. Inevitably, this weakens the position of the reform-oriented groups of the Third World.

The international crisis and the special problems confronting the Third World call forth, as a corollary, a redefinition of the interests of the Western industrial countries in their relations with the South. Historically, a new situation has emerged: Prosperity in the industrial countries of the West, viewed in the context of a free world economy, depends on the increase of mass incomes in the South. The industrial countries of the West are, by themselves, incapable of concerted action to revive demand through rising mass incomes, since some of the weaker countries amongst them have specialised in production lines which face severe competition from the developing countries. Without social structural change and rising mass incomes in the South, it would not be possible in the long run to effect a reduction in the number of working hours and raise mass incomes in the West (to balance out a growing productive capacity, on the one side, and a falling consumptive capacity, on the other).

Strategies to overcome underdevelopment can be implemented with the help of certain sections of the Third World State–classes. There are segments of the State–classes in the South which want to represent the interests of the underprivileged, even if this were only to serve as an instrument to their acquisition or maintenance of power. Meanwhile, tendencies towards the promotion of the private small-scale sector, with the objective of satisfying mass demand, are in evidence even in countries with markedly planned economies. Amongst the State–classes of countries with a strongly inegalitarian income distribution, there are tendencies towards the restriction of high incomes.

The industrial countries of the West must cease to look upon the most conservative groups in a developing country as their most reliable partners, if they wish to cooperate with those segments of the State–classes which are in a position to enforce social structural change. Often, these reformist segments subscribe to the Marxian critique of capitalism. This is only to be expected as long as the industrial countries of the West use the principles of the market economy as a pretext to reject welfare measures in Third World countries, and the redistribution of income on a global scale. Socio-political elements of a social market economy can be found in the development policy and, above all, in the foreign trade policies of industrial countries in very limited sectors. Those Third World groups which proclaim themselves to be socio-revolutionary in nature, and which endorse the Marxist analysis of the development problem, may not be the friends of the USA but, at the same time, need not necessarily be supporters of the USSR. They will be lesser inclined to terminate cooperation with the West, the more the latter supports social structural change towards greater equality. The bourgeois revolution proclaimed the ideals of liberty, equality and fraternity. Investment was remunerative because the lower classes could effect an increase in their incomes in political systems conditioned by these values. Disillusionment with the West in the Third World today is also one of the reasons for these values being represented in an anti-imperialistic and anti-capitalistic terminology. Nevertheless, they clearly remain Western values.

On the foreign policy front, the West would be satisfied with the genuine non-alignment of the countries of the South. For, its economic strength alone would assure it a crucial advantage over the USSR. This advantage will grow once the industrial countries of the West have established, through their pragmatic development policies, that the aid extended by them serves strategies for overcoming underdevelopment through rising mass incomes. Obviously, such a policy should also address the burning political issues of the Third World, particularly the creation of a state for Palestinians in the territories occupied by Israel after 1967, and the reversal of the policy pursued by the apartheid regime of South Africa.

The freedom of the Soviet Union's leeway to extend its sphere of influence is curtailed by the degree to which development strategies catering to the masses can successfully curb internal and inter-state conflict potentials in the South, as well as by the extent to which the implementation of reform policies enables various social groups in the South to adopt non-violent forms of conflict resolution within the overall framework of this process of conflict abatement. The power and influence of the Soviet Union is eroded even in those cases where it had extended invaluable assistance during military conflicts, once concrete development problems emerge. Nicaragua oriented itself to the Soviet Union to the extent it has today only after the West ruled out cooperation based on reform.

The industrial countries of the West may take recourse to two methods to promote the implementation of egalitarist strategies for overcoming underdevelopment. The day-to-day policy of development assistance should accord primacy to those projects which can be integrated into egalitarist production chains, irrespective of the orientation of the governments concerned. The political feasibility of such strategies will be fostered if projects of this type create production capacities which can be utilised even in the event of an expansion of mass demand. No one can speak of 'interference', in contravention of international law, if the governments of the Western industrial countries attach due prominence to such considerations while selecting projects, guaranteeing export credits and promoting investment by the MNCs.

In the context of the West–South dialogue, the industrial countries of the West could utilise the promise of concessions for financing social structural change. $ 10 billion would be sufficient to implement land reforms in the most important countries of the South. Talks on debt restructuring between the Western banks, the IMF and the Third World countries—as in the case of Brazil today—could suggest the possibility of financing a land reform programme instead of demanding the curtailment of public spending.

If the West is to finance a considerable portion of Third World deficit, it can assign this portion to development banks financing projects primarily designed for the labour-intensive production of mass-consumption goods, rather than financing it through balance of payments aid. Even concessions in commodity prices could be linked with agreements on the mode of employment of additional revenue. Duties in industrial countries could also serve as protectionist measures for manufactured exports during an interim period, the revenue from such duties being used to set up egalitarist production chains, or even to finance systems of social insurance in the developing countries.

The South buttresses its demand for a New International Economic Order with the argument that such an order forms part of its efforts to achieve a greater measure of equality and justice. In this respect, the industrial countries of the West should take the South on its word and declare their willingness to make funds available to the South for the eradication of poverty and the development of productive apparatuses used to produce goods for mass consumption.

Such a solution is of definite interest to the people of the industrial countries. The trade unions of the West must realise that it is the unemployed and the poor of the Third World today who go to make up the 'unorganised' sector on the international labour market. Only when these marginalised sections are assured employment through rising mass incomes in the South, will the MNCs be no longer able to avail of an unlimited supply of cheap labour in the South. By promoting strategies for overcoming underdevelopment through rising mass incomes in the South, the West and the South could forge a joint partnership for growth. Mass incomes would rise along with production in the South. In the West, the mechanism crucial to a liberal economy would be preserved, thereby assuring an adjustment between production and demand in the event of an increase in mass incomes, or a reduction in working hours in the West. Such an adjustment would in turn ensure full employment in the West even in case of rising productivity and increasing production of manufactured goods in the Third World.

Select Bibliography

1. Precapitalist Societies in Africa

Coquery-Vidrovitch, Catherine: 'Recherches sur un mode de production africain'. *La Pensée*, (144), March/April 1969; pp. 61–78.

Goody, Jack: *Technology, Tradition and the State in Africa*. London: Oxford University Press, 1971.

Huffman, T.N.: 'The Rise and the Fall of Zimbabwe.' : *Journal of African History*. (13–3), 1972; pp. 353–366.

Mair, Lucy: *Primitive Government. A Study of Traditional Political Systems in Eastern Africa*. Bloomington: Indiana University Press, 1977.

Maquet, Jacques: *Les civilisations noires. Histoire, techniques, arts, societes*. Vervien: Marabout, 1977.

Suret-Canale, Jean: 'Les sociétés traditionnelles en Afrique et le concept de mode de production asiatique'. *La Pensée* (117), October 1964; pp. 21–42.

2. 'Asiatic Modes of Production'

Chesneaux, Jean: 'Le mode de production asiatique, quelques perspectives de recherche'. *La Pensée* (114), March/April 1964; pp.33–55.

Junge, Peter: *Asiatische Produktionsweise und Staatsentstehung.: Zum Problem der logischen Analyse der Staatsentstehung mit Gemeineigentum*. Bremen: Übersee–Museum, Bremen, 1980.

Reischauer, Edwin O and Fairbank, John K.: *East Asia: The Great Tradition*. Boston: Houghton Mifflin, 1960.

Tökei, Ferenc: *Sur le mode de production asiatique*. Budapest: Akadémiai Kiadó, 1966.

Wittfogel, Karl August: *Oriental Despotism: A Comparative Study of Total Power*. New Haven: Yale University Press, 1957.

3. The Industrial Revolution in Great Britain

Botham, F.W. and Hunt, E.H.: 'Wages in Britain During the Industrial Revolution'. *The Economic History Review*. (40–3), 1987; pp. 380–399.

Deane, Phyllis and Cole, W.A.: *British Economic Growth, 1688–1959: Trends and Structures*. Cambridge: Cambridge University Press, 1967.

Flinn, M.W.: 'Trends in Real Wages', 1750–1850. *Economic History Review*. (28–3),1975; pp. 395–413.

Hartwell, Richard M.: *The Industrial Revolution and Economic Growth*. London: Methuen, 1971.
Jones, Eric L.: *Agriculture and the Industrial Revolution*. Oxford: Basil Blackwell, 1974.
Musson, Albert E.: *The Growth of British Industry*. London: Batsford, 1978.
Rowlands, Marie B.: *Masters and Men in the West Midland Metalware Trades Before the Industrial Revolution*. Manchester: Manchester University Press, 1975.
Thirsk, Joan: *Economic Policy and Projects. The Development of a Consumer Society in Early Modern England*. Oxford: Clarendon Press, 1978.

4. The Analysis of the Capitalist World-System

Elsenhans, Hartmut: 'Grundlagen der Entwicklung der kapitalistischen Weltwirtschaft' in Senghaas, Dieter, (ed.): *Kapitalistische Weltökonomie. Kontroversen über ihren Ursprung und ihre Entwicklungsdynamik*. Frankfurt: Suhrkamp, 1979; pp. 103-150.
Frank, André Gunder: *Dependent Accumulation and Underdevelopment*. London: Macmillan, 1978.
Wallerstein, Immanuel Maurice: *The Modern World-System, I. Capitalist Agriculture and the Origins of the European World-Economy in the Sixteenth Century*. New York: Academic Press, 1974.
Wallerstein, Immanuel Maurice: *The Modern World-System, II. Mercantilism and the Consolidation of the European World-Economy, 1600-150*. New York: Academic Press, 1980.

5. The History of Slavery

Aykroyd, W.R.: *Sweet Malefactor. Sugar; Slavery and Human Society*. London: Heinemann, 1967.
Blake, W.O.: *The History of Slavery and the Slave Trade. Ancient and Modern. The Forms of Slavery that Prevailed in Ancient Nations Particularly in Greece and Rome. The African Slave Trade and the Political History of Slavery in the United States. Compiled with Authentic Materials*. Columbus, Ohio: J.H. Miller, 1858.
Curtin, Philip D.: *The Atlantic Slave Trade*. Wisconsin: Madison University Press, 1969.
Davidson, Basil: *The African Slave Trade: Precolonial History 1450-1850*. Boston: Little & Brown, 1961.
Fogel, Robert William and Engerman, Stanley L.: *Time on the Cross: The Economics of American Negro Slavery*. Boston: Little & Brown, 1974.
Genovese, Eugene D.: *From Rebellion to Revolution: Afro-American Revolts in the Making of the Modern World*. Baton Rouge: Louisiana State University Press, 1979.
Kopytoff, Igor and Miers, Suzanne, eds.: *Slavery in Africa: Historical and Anthropological Perspectives*. Madison, Wisc.: University of Wisconsin Press, 1977.
Nieboer, Herman Jeremias: *Slavery as an Industrial System*. The Hague: Nijhoff, 1900.
Williams, Eric: *Capitalism and Slavery*. London: Andre Deutsch, 1964.

6. Forms of Labour in Colonial Latin America

Bagú, Sergio: *Economía de la sociedad colonial: Ensayo de historia comparada de América Latina.* Buenos Aires: El Ateneo, 1949.

Bannon, John Francis, ed.: *Indian Labor in the Spanish Indies. Was There Another Solution?.* Boston: D.C. Heath, 1966.

Borah, Woodrow: *New Spain's Century of Depression.* Berkeley: University of California Press, 1951.

Simpson, Lesley Bird: *The Encomienda in New Spain.* Berkeley: University of California Press, 1950.

Zavala, Silvio A.: *La encomienda indiana.* Madrid: Centro de Estudios Historicos, 1935

7. Resistance upto the Close of the Nineteenth Century

Chesneaux, Jean and Bastid, Marianne: *Des guerres de l'opium à la guerre franco–indochinoise, 1840–1855.* Paris: Hattier, 1969.

Chesneaux, Jean, ed.: *Popular Movements and Secret Societies in China, 1840–1950.* Stanford, Calif.: Stanford University Press, 1972.

Cipolla, Carlo M.: *Guns and Sails in the Early Phase of European Expansion, 1400–1700.* London: Collins, 1965.

Crowder, Michael, ed.: *West African Resistance: The Military Response to Colonial Occupation.* New York: Africana Publishing Co., 1971.

Feuerwerker, Albert: *China's Early Industrialisation.* Cambridge, Mass.: Harvard University Press, 1958.

Jara, Alvaro: *Guerre et société au Chili. Essai de sociologie coloniale. La transformation de la guerre d'Araucanie et l'esclavage des Indiens du début de la conquête espagnole aux débuts de l'esclavage légal (1612).* Paris: Institut des Hautes Etudes de l'Amérique Latine, 1961.

Mannoni, Dominique O.: *Prospero and Caliban. The Psychology of Colonisation.* London: Methuen, 1956.

Pereira de Queiroz, Maria Isaura: *Réforme et révolution dans les sociétés traditionnelles: Histoire et ethnologie des mouvements messianiques.* Paris: Anthropos, 1968.

8. Colonialism in the Nineteenth and Twentieth Centuries

Albertini, Rudolf von: *Europäische Kolonialherrschaft 1880–1940.* Zurich: Atlantis, 1976.

Feis, Herbert: *Europe: the World's Banker 1870–1914: An Account of European Foreign Investment and the Connection of World Finance With Diplomacy Before the War.* New Haven: Yale University Press, 1930.

Fieldhouse, David Kenneth: *The Colonial Empires. A Contemporary Survey from the Eighteenth Century.* London: Weidenfeld & Nicolson, 1966.

Ganiage, Jean: *L'expansion coloniale de la France sous la IIIe République 1871–1914.* Paris: Payot, 1968.

Gann, Lewis H. and Duignan, Peter, eds.: *Colonialism in Africa 1870–1960, Vol. 1: The History and Politics of Colonialism, 1870–1914.* Cambridge: Cambridge University Press, 1969.

Gann, Lewis H. and Duignan, Peter, eds.: *Colonialism in Africa 1870–1960, Vol. 2: The History and Politics of Colonialism, 1914–1960*. Cambridge: Cambridge University Press, 1970.

9. Anti-colonial Resistance and the Dissolution of the Colonial Empires

Cabral, Amilcar: *Revolution in Guinea*. New York: Monthly Review Press, 1970.

Chaliand, Gérard: *Revolution in the Third World: Myth and Prospects*. Haddocks: Harvester Press, 1977.

Davidson, Basil: *The People's Cause: A History of Guerillas in Africa*. Harlow: Longmann, 1981.

Fanon, Frantz: *The Wretched of the Earth*. New York: Grove Press, 1965.

Gann, Lewis H.: *Guerillas in History*. Stanford: Hoover Institution Press. Stanford University, 1971.

Gott, Richard: *Guerilla Movements in Latin America*. London: Nelson, 1970.

Johnson, Chalmers A.: *Peasant Nationalism and Communist Power: The Emergence of Revolutionary China 1937–1945*. Stanford: Stanford University Press, 1962.

Leites, Nathan and Wolf, Charles jr.: *Rebellion and Authority*. Chicago: Markham, 1970.

Mao Tse-tung: *Strategic Problems of China's Revolutionary War*. Bombay: People's Publishing House, 1951.

Turner, Victor, ed.: *Colonialism in Africa, 1870–1960, Vol. 3: Profiles of Change: African Society and Colonial Rule*. London: Cambridge University Press, 1971.

10. Agrarian Problems in the Third World

Ahmed, Iftikhar: *Technological Change and Agrarian Structure: A Study of Bangladesh*. Geneva: ILO, 1981.

Berry, Albert R. and Cline, William R., eds.: *Agrarian Structure and Productivity*. Baltimore: Johns Hopkins, 1979.

Bhalla, G.S. and Chadha, S.K.: *Green Revolution and the Small Peasant: A Study of Income Distribution among Punjab Cultivators*. New Delhi: Concept Publishing Company, 1983.

Chonchol, Jacques: *Paysans à venir: Les sociétés rurales du Tiers-Monde*. Paris: La découverte, 1986.

Clayton, Eric: *Agriculture, Poverty and Freedom in Developing Countries*. London: Macmillan, 1983.

Dorner, Peter, ed.: *Land Reform in Latin America: Issues and Cases*. Madison, Wisc.: Land Economics, 1971.

Elsenhans, Hartmut: 'Agrarverfassung, Akkumulationsprozeß, Demokratisierung', in Elsenhans, Hartmut, ed.: *Agrarreform in der Dritten Welt*. Frankfurt: Campus, 1979; pp. 505-652.

Fuhr, Harald: *Bauern und Parteifunktionäre: Eine Untersuchung zur politischen Dynamik des peruanischen Agrarsektors, 1969–1981*. Saarbrücken: Breitenbach, 1987.

Geertz, Clifford: *Agricultural Involution. The Processes of Ecological Change in Indonesia*. Berkeley: University of California Press, 1963.

Ghose, Ajit Kumar, ed.: *Agrarian Reform in Contemporary Developing Countries.* London: Croom Helm, 1983.

Ip, P.C. and Stahl, C.W.: 'Systems of Land Tenure: Allocative Efficiency and Economic Development'. *American Journal of Agricultural Economics* (60–1), February 1978; pp. 19–28.

Islam, Rizwanul, ed.: *Strategies for Alleviating Poverty in Rural Asia.* Dhaka, Bangkok: Bangladesh Institute of Development Studies/International Labour Organisation—Asian Employment Programme, 1985.

Jain, L.C., Krishnamurty, B.V. and Tripathy, P.M.: *Grass Without Roots: Rural Development under Government Auspices.* New Delhi: Sage, 1985.

Migdal, Joel S.: *Peasants, Politics and Revolution: Pressures Toward Political and Social Change in the Third World.* Princeton: Princeton University Press, 1974.

Paige, Jeffery M.: *Agrarian Revolution: Social Movements and Export Agriculture in the Underdeveloped World.* London: Free Press, 1975.

Popkin, Samuel L.: *The Rational Peasant: The Political Economy of Rural Society in Vietnam.* Berkeley: University of California Press, 1979.

Sternberg, Marvin J.: *Agrarian Reform and Employment.* Geneva: ILO (International Labour Office), 1971.

Tai, Hung–Chao: *Land Reform and Politics: A Comparative Analysis.* Berkeley: University of California Press, 1974.

Wolf, Eric R.: *Peasant Wars in Twentieth Century.* New York: Harper & Row, 1968.

11. The Labour Movement in the Third World

Cohen, Michael A.: *Urban Policy and Political Conflict in Africa: A Study of the Ivory Coast.* Chicago: University of Chicago Press, 1974.

Cohen, Robin: *Labour and Politics in Nigeria, 1945–1971.* London: Heinemann, 1974.

Cox, Robert W.: 'Labor and Hegemony'. *International Organization* (31–2), Spring 1977; pp. 385–424.

Deyo, Frederick C.: *Dependent Development and Industrial Order: An Asian Case Study.* New York: Praeger, 1981.

Luke, David F.: *Labour and Parastatal Politics in Sierra Leone: A Study of African Working–class Ambivalence.* Lanham, New York, London: University Press of America, 1984.

Luther, Hans Ulrich: 'The Repression of Labour Protest in Singapore: Unique Case or Future Model?'. *Development and Change,* (10–2), April 1979; pp. 287–299.

Mazrui, A.A. and Rotberg, R., Hrsg.: *Protest and Power in Black Africa.* London: Oxford University Press, 1970.

Peace, Adrian I.: *Choice, Class and Conflict: A Study of Southern Nigerian Factory Workers.* Brighton: Harvest Press, 1979.

Petras, James and Zeitlin, Maurice: 'Miners and Agrarian Radicalism'. *American Sociological Review* (32–4), August 1967; pp. 578-586.

Sandbrook, Richard and Cohen, Robin, eds.: *The Development of an African Working Class: Studies in Class Formation and Action.* London: Longman, 1975.

Waterman, Peter: 'Workers in the Third World'. *Monthly Review* (29–4), September 1977; pp. 51–64.

12. The 'New' Middle Class and the Military

Brass, Paul R. and Franda, Marcus F., eds.: *Radical Politics in South Asia.* Cambridge, Mass.: MIT Press, 1973.

Halpern, Manfred: 'Egypt and the New Middle Class: Reaffirmations and New Explorations',. *Comparative Studies in Society and History*(11–1), January 1969; pp. 97–108.

Markakis, John: *Ethiopia : Anatomy of a Traditional Polity.* Oxford: Clarendon Press, 1974.

Nordlinger, Eric A.: *Soldiers in Politics: Military Coups and Governments.* Englewood Cliffs, N.J.: Prentice Hall, 1977.

Odetola, Theophilus O.: *Military Regimes and Development: A Comparative Analysis of African States.* London: George Allen & Unwin, 1982.

Pabanel, Jean-Pierre: *Les coups d'etat militaires en Afrique Noire.* Paris: Harmattan, 1984.

Perlmutter, Amos: 'The New Middle-Class in Egypt'. *Comparative Studies in Society and History* (10–1), October 1967; pp. 45–65.

Silva Michelena, José Augustin: *The Illusion of Democracy in Dependent Nations.* Cambridge, Mass.: M.I.T. Press, 1971.

Smith, Anthony D.: *Theories of Nationalism.* London: Duckworth, 1971.

Smith, Peter H.: *Labyrinths of Power: Political Recruitment in Twentieth-Century Mexico.* Princeton: Princeton University Press, 1979.

13. The Third World State

Adamolekun, Ladipo: *Politics and Administration in Nigeria.* Ibadan: Spectrum Books, 1986.

Ayubi, Nazih N. M.: *Bureaucracy and Politics in Contemporary Egypt.* London: Ithaca Press 1980.

Callaghy, Thomas M.: *The State–Society Struggle: Zaire in Comparative Perspective.* New York: Columbia University Press, 1984.

Elsenhans, Hartmut: *Abhängiger Kapitalismus oder bürokratische Entwicklungsgesellschaft. Versuch über den Staat in der Dritten Welt.* Frankfurt: Campus, 1981.

Elsenhans, Hartmut: 'Public Administration in Developing Countries: Specificities of "Public" and "Administration" in Market-Regulated Developing and Capitalistic Societies'. *Indian Journal of Public Administration* (35–1), January–March 1989; pp. 16–26.

Evans, Peter B.: *Dependent Development: The Alliance of Multinational, State and Local Capital in Brazil.* Princeton: Princeton University Press, 1979.

Girling, John L.S.: *The Bureaucratic Polity in Modernising Societies: Similarities, Differences and Prospects in the ASEAN Region.* Singapore: Institute of South East Asian Studies, 1981.

Grindle, Merilee Serill: *Bureaucrats, Politicians, and Peasants in Mexico: A Case Study in Public Policy.* Berkeley: University of California Press, 1977.

Hyden, Goran: *No Shortcuts to Progress: African Development Management in Perspective.* London: Heinemann, 1983.

Jackson, Robert Harry and Rosberg, Carl Gustav: *Personal Rule in Black Africa: Prince, Autocrat, Prophet, Tyrant.* Berkeley: University of California Press, 1982.

Jain, R.B. and Chaudhuri, P.N.: *Bureaucratic Values in Development*. New Delhi: Uppal Publishing House, 1982.

Jain, R.B., ed.: *Bureaucratic Politics in the Third World*. New Delhi: Gitanjali, 1989.

Kohli, Atul: *The State and Poverty in India: Three Politics of Reform*. Cambridge: Cambridge University Press, 1987.

Murray, Roger: 'Second Thoughts on Ghana'. *New Left Review*, (45) March/April 1967; pp. 25–39.

Riggs, Fred W.: *Administration in Developing Countries : The Theory of Prismatic Society*. Boston: Houghton-Mifflin Company, 1964.

Saul, John S.: 'The State in Post-Colonial Societies'. *Socialist Register* (11), 1974; pp. 349–372.

Saulniers, Alfred H.: *Economic and Political Roles in the State in Latin America*. Austin: University of Texas, 1985.

Sklar, Richard.: 'Political Science and National Integration: A Radical Approach'. *Jornal of Modern African Studies* (5–1), 1967, p. 8.

Sloan, John: 'Bureaucracy and Public Policy in Latin America'. *Inter-American Economic Affairs* (34–4), Spring 1981; pp. 17–47.

Thomas, Clive Y.: *The Rise of the Authoritarian State in Peripheral Societies*. London: Heinemann, 1984.

14. The Theory of Modernisation

Hirschman, Albert O.: *The Strategy of Economic Development*. New Haven: Yale University Press, 1958.

Leibenstein, Harvey: *Economic Backwardness and Economic Growth*. New York: John Wiley, 1960.

Meier, Gerald M.: *Leading Issues in Development Economics: Selected Materials and Commentary*. New York: Oxford University Press, 1964.

Nurkse, Ragnar: *Problems of Capital Formation in Underdeveloped Countries*. New York: Oxford University Press, 1953.

Rosenstein, P. N.: 'Problems of Industrialisation of Eastern and South Eastern Europe'. *Economic Journal*(53–210), June/September 1943; pp. 202–211.

15. Terms of Trade and Improvement in Commodity Prices

Benachenhou, Abdellatif: 'Le renversement de la problématique ricardienne des coûts comparés dans la théorie économique contemporaine'. *Revue algérienne des sciences juridiques, économiques et politiques* (8–4), December 1971; pp. 913–934.

Elsenhans, Hartmut: 'Le monde arabe et l'Europe dans la nouvelle division internationale du travail', in Khader, Bichara, (ed.): *Coopération Euro–Arabe: Diagnostique et Prospective. Actes du Colloque organisé à Louvain-la-Neuve (2–4 décembre 1982) par le Centre d'Etude et de Recherche sur le Monde Arabe Contemporain de l'Université Catholique de Louvain*. Volume 3. Louvain-la-Neuve: CERMAC 1983; pp. 34-123.

Emmanuel, Arghiri: *Unequal Exchange*. London: New Left Books, 1972.

Ford, A. G.: 'Export–Price Indices for the Argentine Republic, 1881–1914'. *Inter-American Economic Affairs* (9–2), Autumn 1955; pp. 42–54.

Imlah, Albert H.: 'The Terms of Trade of the United Kingdom, 1798–1913.' *Journal of Economic History* (10–2), November 1950; pp. 170–194.

Mahajan, V. S.: 'The Terms of Trade Between Primary Producing and Manufacturing Countries and Economic Development.' *Indian Journal of Economics*, (40–159), April 1960; pp. 357–360.

Peláez, Carlos Manuel: 'The Theory and Reality of Imperialism in the Coffee Economy of Nineteenth Century Brasil.' *Economic History Review* (29–2), 1976; pp. 276–290.

Prebisch, Raul: 'The Economic Development of Latin America and its Principal Problems'. *Economic Bulletin for Latin America*. (7–1), February 1962; pp.1–22.

Sen, Nabendu: 'India's Terms of Trade, 1871–72 to 1892–93'. *Economic and Political Weekly* (11–46), November 13th, 1976; pp. 1975–1803.

Sid Ahmed, Abdelkader: *Économie de l'industrialisation à partir de ressources naturelles* (I. B. R.). Paris: Publisud, 1989.

Singer, Hans W.: 'US Foreign Investment in Underdeveloped Areas. The Distribution of Gains between Investing and Borrowing Countries'. *The American Economic Review* (40–2), May 1950; pp. 473–485.

United Nations: *Relative Prices of Exports and Imports of Underdeveloped Countries.* New York: United Nations, 1949.

16. Commodity Production in the Third World

Coale, William Davis: *West German Transnationals in Tropical Africa: The Case of Liberia and the Bong Mining Company.* Ann Arbor, Mich.: Doctoral Thesis, Boston University, 1977.

Elsenhans, Hartmut, ed.: *Erdöl für Europa.* Hamburg: Hoffmann & Campe, 1974.

Giraud, Pierre-Noël: *Géopolitique des ressources minières.* Paris: Economica, 1983.

Levin, Jonathan V.: *The Export Economies. Their Patterns of Development in Historical Perspective.* Cambridge: Harvard University Press, 1960.

Nankani, Gobind: *Development Problems of Mineral-Exporting Countries.* World Bank Staff Working Paper No. 354. Washington: World Bank, 1979.

Navin, Thomas R.: *Copper Mining and Management.* Tucson, Arizona: University of Arizona Press, 1978.

Radetzki, Marian: 'Changing Structures in the Financing of the Minerals Industry in LDCs'. *Development and Change* (11–1), January 1980; pp. 1–16.

Radetzki, Marian: 'Has Political Risk Scared Mineral Investment Away From the Deposits in Developing Countries'. *World Development* (10–1), January 1982; pp. 39-48.

The Role of the State Enterprises in the Solid Minerals Industry in Developing Countries. Special Issue of Raw Materials Report. Stockholm, 1989.

Sideri, Sandro and Johns, Sheridan, eds.: *Mining for Development in the Third World. Multinational Corporations, State Enterprises and the International Economy.* New York: Pergamon Press, 1980.

17. The Theory of Imperialism

Amin, Samir: *Unequal Development: An Essay on the Social Formation of Peripherical Capitalism.* Haddocks: Harvester Press, 1976.

Dutt, Rajani P.: *India Today.* Bombay: People's Publishing House, 1949.

Elsenhans, Hartmut: 'Egalitarisme social et critique des modes de production dans la périphérie au lieu d'antiimpérialisme et critique des rapports économiques entre le centre et la périphérie', in: *EADI Working Group: Multinationales et Développement: un débat. Symposium de Paris du 10 octobre 1980.* Paris: Université de Paris, Institut d'Etudes du Développement Economique et Social, 1981; pp. 1–71.

Galeano, Eduardo H.: *Las venas abiertas de América Latina.* Montevideo: Universidad Nacional de la República, 1971.

Lenin, Vladimir Illich: *Imperialism, the Highest Stage of Capitalism.* Moscow: Foreign Languages Publication, 1917.

Luxemburg, Rosa: *The Accumulation of Capital.* London: Routledge & Kegan Paul, 1951.

Rodney, Walter: *How Europe Underdeveloped Africa.* London: Bogle-L'Ouverture Publications, 1972.

18. The Theory of Dependency

Cardoso, Fernando Henrique and Faletto, Enzo: *Dependencia y desarrollo en América Latina.* Documentos Teoricos Nr.1. Lima: Instituto de Estudios Peruanos, 1967.

Cardoso, Fernando Henrique: *Sociologie du développement en Amérique latine.* Paris: Anthropos, 1973.

Cardoso, Fernando H.: 'The Consumption of Dependency Theory in the United States'. *Latin American Research Review* (12–3), 1977; pp. 7–24.

Frank, André Gunder: Capitalism and Underdevelopment in Latin America: Historial Studies of Chile and Brazil. New York: Monthly Review Press, 1969.

Furtado, Celso: *Le mythe du développement économique.* Paris: Anthropos, 1976.

Sunkel, Osvaldo: *El subdesarrollo latinoamericano y la teoria del desarrollo.* Mexico: Siglo Veintuno Editores, 1970.

19. Critical Appraisals of the Theory of Dependency

Elsenhans, Hartmut: 'Dependencia, Underdevelopment and the Third World State'. *Law and State.* (36), 1987; pp. 65–94.

Lall, Sanjaya: 'Is Dependencê a Useful Concept in Analysing Underdevelopment?' *World Development.* (3–11/12), November/December 1975; pp. 799–810.

Palma, Gabriel: Dependency: A Formal Theory of Underdevelopment or a Methodology for the Analysis of Concrete Situations of Underdevelopment. *World Development* (6–7/8), July/August 1978; pp. 881–924.

Ramos, Joseph: 'A Heterodoxical Interpretation of the Employment Problem in Latin America'. *World Development* (2–7), July 1974; pp. 47–58.

Warren, Bill: *Imperialism: Pioneer of Capitalism.* London: NLB, 1980.

20. Import–substituting Industrialisation

Ahmad, Jaleel: *Import Substitution: Trade and Development.* Greenwich, Conn.: JAI Press, 1978.

Bruton, Henry J.: 'The Import-Substitution Strategy of Economic Development: A Survey. *Pakistan Development Review*(10–2), Summer 1970; pp. 123–146.

Hirschman, Albert O.: 'The Political Economy of Import Substituting Industrialisation in Latin America'. *Quarterly Journal of Economics*(82–1), February 1968; pp. 1-32.

Leff, Nathaniel H.: *Economic Policy Making and Development in Brazil.* New York: John Wiley & Sons, 1968.

Schmitz, Hubert: 'Industrialisation Strategies in Less Developed Countries: Some Lessons of Historical Experience'. *Journal of Development Studies,*(21–1), October 1984; pp. 1–21.

21. Export-oriented Industrialisation

Cline, William R. 'Can the East Asian Model of Development Be Generalised?' *World Development,* (10–2), February 1982; pp. 81–90.

Elsenhans, Hartmut: 'Social Consequences of the NIEO. Structural Change in the Periphery as Precondition for Continual Reforms in the Centre,' in: Jahn, Egbert, and Sakamoto Yoshikazu, eds.: *Elements of World Instability: Armaments, Communication, Food, International Division of Labour, Proceedings of the International Peace Research Association. Eighth General Conference.* Frankfurt: Campus, 1981; pp. 86–95.

Elsenhans, Hartmut: 'Absorbing Global Surplus Labor'. *Annals of the American Academy of Political and Social Science* (492), July 1987; pp. 124–135.

Hamilton, Clive: *Capitalist Industrialisation in Korea.* Boulder (Col.): Westview, 1985.

Lee, Eddy, ed.: *Export-Led Industrialisation and Development.* Geneva: ILO, 1981.

Renshaw, Geoffrey, ed.: *Employment, Trade and North–South Cooperation.* Geneva: ILO, 1981.

Saunders, Christopher, ed.: *The Political Economy of New and Old Industrial Countries.* London: Buttersworth, 1981.

Yi, Guk-Yueng: *Staat und Kapitalakkumulation in ostasiatischen Ländern: Ein Vergleich zwischen Korea und Taiwan.* Saarbrucken: Breitenbach, 1988.

22. Public Enterprises

Badawi, Ibrahim Mohammed: *Organisation and Administration of Public Enterprises for Socio-Economic Development: The Egyptian Experiences 1805–1975.* Doctoral Thesis. New York: University of New York, 1977.

Boneo, Horacio: *Saber ver las Empresas Publicas.* Ciudad Universitaria Rodrigo Facio (Costa Rica): Editorial Universitaria Centroamericana (EDUCA), 1980.

Clark, W. Edmund: *Socialist Development and Public Investment in Tanzania, 1964–73.* Toronto: University of Toronto Press, 1978.

Guru, Damodar D. and Ahsan, Qamar: *Public Enterprise with Special Reference to India.* Delhi: Amar Prakashan, 1987.

Saulniers, Alfred H., ed.: *The Public Sector in Latin América.* Austin: University of Texas, 1984.

Sloan, John W.: *Public Policy in Latin America: A Comparative Survey.* Pittsburgh (Pa.): University of Pittsburgh Press, 1984.

Sobhan, Rehman: 'Public Enterprises and the Nature of the State'. *Development and Change,* (10–1), January 1979; pp. 23–40.

Sobhan, Rehman: *Public Enterprises and the Nature of the State: The Case of South Asia.* Dhaka: Centre for Social Studies, 1983.

Toye, John: *Public Expenditure and Indian Development Policy, 1960–1970.* Cambridge: Cambridge University Press, 1981.

23. Third World Debt

Abbott, George C.: *International Indebtedness and the Developing Countries.* London: Croom Helm, 1979.

Branford, Sue and Kucinski, Bernardo: *The Debt Squads: The US, the Banks and Latin America.* London: ZED Books, 1988.

Cline, William R.: *International Debt: Systemic Risk and Policy Response.* Cambridge, Mass.: M.I.T. Press, 1984.

Elsenhans, Hartmut: 'Endettement: Echec d'une industrialisation du Tiers Monde'. *Tiers Monde* (25–99), July/September 1984; pp. 551–564.

Frieden, Jeff: 'Third World Indebted Industrialisation: International Finance and State Capitalism in Mexico, Brazil, Algeria and South Korea'. *International Organisation* (35–3), Summer 1981; pp. 407–432.

Friedman, Irving S.: *The World Debt Dilemma: Managing Country Risk.* Washington: Council for International Banking Studies, 1983.

Gern, Jean-Pierre: 'Le developpement de L'Afrique confronté aux politiques d'ajustement structurel. Neuchâtel: EDES, 1987.

Killick, Tony: *The Quest for Economic Stabilisation: The IMF and the Third World.* London: Heinemann, 1984.

Körner, Peter, et al.: *The IMF and the Debt Crisis: A Guide to the Third World's Dilemma.* London: ZED Books, 1986.

Payer, Cheryl: *The Debt Trap: The IMF and the Third World.* Harmondsworth: Penguin, 1974.

Versluysen, Eugene L.: *The Political Economy of International Finance.* West-mead: Gower, 1981.

Wionczek, Miguel S., ed.: *LDC External Debt and the World Economy.* Mexico: El Colegio de México, 1978.

24. The Technology Issue and Transfer of Technology

Chudnovsky, Daniel, Nagao, Masafumi, and Jacobson, Staffan: *Capital Goods Production in the Third World: An Economic Study of Technology Acquisition.* London: Frances Pinter, 1983.

Dahlman, Carl J. and Sercovich, Francisco: *Local Development and Exports of*

Technology: The Comparative Advantage of Argentina, Brazil, India, the Republic of Korea, and Mexico. World Bank Staff Working Paper No. 667. Washington, D.C.: World Bank, 1984.

Edquist, Charles: *Capitalism, Socialism and Technology.* New York: ZED Books, 1985.

Elsenhans, Hartmut: 'Der Mythos der Kapitalintensität und die notwendig falsche Technologiewahl der Entwicklungsländer', in: Kohler-Koch, Beate, ed.: *Technik und internationale Entwicklung.* Baden-Baden: Nomos, 1986; pp. 267–319.

Emmanuel, Arghiri: *Appropriate or Underdeveloped Technology? Followed by a Discussion with Celso Furtado and Hartmut Elsenhans.* Chichester: John Wiley, 1982.

Ernst, Dieter, ed.: *The New International Division of Labour, Technology, and Underdevelopment: Consequences for the Third World.* Frankfurt: Campus, 1980.

Jacobsson, Staffan and Sigurdson, Jon, eds.: *Technological Trends and Challenges in Electronics: Dominance of the Industrialised World and Responses in the Third World.* Lund: Research Policy Institute, University of Lund, 1983.

Jécquier, Nicolas and Blanc, Gérard: *The World of Appropriate Technology: A Quantitative Analysis.* Paris: OECD, 1983.

Judet, Pierre, Kahn, Philippe and Kiss, Alexandre, eds.: *Transfert de technologie et développement.* Paris: Librairie Technique, 1977.

Sen, Amartiya Kumar: *Choice of Techniques: An Aspect of the Theory of Planned Economic Development.* Oxford: Basil Blackwell, 1968.

Stewart, Frances and James, Jeffrey: *The Economics of New Technology in Developing Countries.* London: Frances Pinter, 1982.

Westphal, Larry E., Kim, Linsu and Dahlman, Carl J.: *Reflections on Korea's Acquisition of Technology.* Washington, D.C.: World Bank, 1984.

25. Transnational Corporations and Capital Export

Barnet, Richard and Müller, Ronald: *Global Reach: The Power of the Multinational Corporation.* New York: Simon & Schuster, 1974.

Bornschier, Volker and Chase-Dunn, Christopher: *Transnational Corporations and Underdevelopment.* New York: Praeger, 1985.

Grou, Pierre: *The Financial Structure of Multinational Capitalism.* Leamington Spa: Berg, 1985.

International Labour Office: *Employment Effects of Multinational Enterprises in Developing Countries.* Geneva: ILO, 1981.

Jodice, David A.: 'Sources of Change in Third World Regimes for Foreign Direct Investment, 1968–1976'. *International Organisation* (34–1), Spring 1980; pp. 177–206.

Kragenau, Henry: *Internationale Direktinvestitionen.* Hamburg: Weltarchiv, 1987.

Krasner, Stephen D.: 'US Commercial and Monetary Policy: Unraveling the Paradox of External Strength and Internal Weakness'. *International Organisation* (31–3), Autumn 1977; pp. 635–671.

Newfarmer, Richard S.: *Profits, Progress and Poverty: Case Studies of International Industries in Latin America.* Notre Dame, Indiana: University of Notre Dame Press, 1985.

Rubin, Seymour J.: 'The Multinational Enterprise at Bay'. *American Journal of International Law* (68–3), July 1974; pp. 475–488.

Vernon, Raymond: *Sovereignty at Bay. The Multinational Spread of US Enterprises.* London: Longman, 1971.

Vernon, Raymond: *Storm Over the Multinationals.* Cambridge, Mass.: Harvard University Press, 1977.

Wilkens, Mira: *The Maturing of Multinational Enterprise: American Business Abroad From 1914 to 1970.* Cambridge, Mass.: Harvard University Press, 1974.

26. Third World Organisations

Cizelj, Boris, eds.: *The Challenges of South–South Cooperation.* Boulder, Col.: Westview, 1983.

Guitard, Odette: *Bandoeng et le réveil des peuples colonisés.* Paris: Presses Universitaires de France, 1969.

Mates, Leo: *Non-Alignment: Theory and Current Policy.* Dobbs Ferry: Oceana, 1972.

Rothstein, Robert L.: *Global Bargaining. UNCTAD and the Quest for a New International Economic Order.* Princeton: Princeton University Press, 1979.

Sauvant, Karl Peter: *The Group of 77: Evolution, Structure, Organisation.* New York: Oceana, 1981.

Shaw, Timothy M. and Aluko, Olajide, eds.: *The Political Economy of African Foreign Policy.* Aldershot: Gower, 1984.

Willetts, Peter: *The Non-Aligned Movement: The Origins of a Third World Alliance.* London: Frances Pinter, 1978.

27. Statistical References

Annual Report. International Monetary Fund. Washington.

Balance of Payments Yearbook. International Monetary Fund. Washington (Annual). Standardised data on the balance of payment of all member countries.

Demographic Yearbook. United Nations. New York (annual).

Direction of Trade Statistics. International Monetary Fund. Washington (annual). Total trade data by region and not by merchandise group.

FAO Production Yearbook. Food and Agriculture Organisation of the United Nations. Rome (annual). Data on output and yield, by individual countries and country groups.

Federal Bureau of Statistics (Statistisches Bundesamt Wiesbaden), General Statistics on Foreign Countries. Surveys and summaries on several Third World countries in irregular order.

Handbook of International Trade and Development Statistics. UNCTAD. Geneva (annual). Production and trade data for developing countries.

International Financial Statistics. International Monetary Fund. Washington (monthly). The most important indicators of the economic development of all member countries and the development of the most important commodity prices.

Monthly Bulletin of Statistics. United Nations. New York (monthly). With annual overviews of different areas with monthly variations.

OECD. Co-operation for Development. Policies and Contribution of the Members of the Committee for Development Aid. Paris (annual). Development aid and public and private capital flows along with an overview of the economic situation of the Third World.

OECD. Financing and External Debt of Developing Countries. Paris (annual).

Statistical Yearbook. United Nations. New York (annual).

US Direct Investment Abroad: Annual Report, in: *Survey of Current Business (various issues).*

World Debt Tables. World Bank. Washington (annual).

World Development Report. World Bank. Washington (annual). Important indicators for the economic development of the developing countries and outlines of problem issues specific to each year.

World Economic Survey. United Nations. New York (annual).

Yearbook of Industrial Statistics. General Industrial Statistics/Commodity Production Data. United Nations. New York (annual).

Yearbook of International Trade Statistics. United Nations. New York (annual).

Yearbook of Labour Statistics. International Labour Office. Geneva (annual). The unemployed and employed, by production sectors and branches in individual countries.

Yearbook of National Accounts Statistics. United Nations. New York (annual).

Yearbook of World Energy Statistics. United Nations. New York (annual).